Postcards from Lonnie

Postcards from Lonnie

How I Rediscovered My Brother on the
Street Corner He Called Home

Lisa Johnson

Rand-Smith Publishing
Ashland, VA USA

While this book is based on a true story, some of the names and identifying details have been changed to protect the privacy of individuals.

POSTCARDS FROM LONNIE: How I Rediscovered My Brother on the Street Corner He Called Home

Copyright 2020

By Lisa Johnson

Print ISBN: 978-1-950544-13-4

Digital ISBN: 978-1-950544-14-1

Cover photos are from the author's personal collection.

Rand-Smith Publishing

www.Rand-Smith.com

Ashland, Va

Printed in the USA

Contents

Introduction *1*

1. February/March 1994   7

2. April 1994   *36*

3. June 1994   *66*

4. July 1994   *89*

5. August 1994   *114*

6. November 1994   *135*

7. January/February 1998   *147*

8. March 1998   *166*

Introduction

The loss of my brother, Lonnie, undid me, probably because so much was unfinished between us, and, as I believed at the time, between Lonnie and the universe. I remain undone, maybe permanently.

Lonnie, on the other hand, in life and in death, seemed to take whatever came along in good faith, not asking much of each day. When he died in February 2005, a few weeks after his 58th birthday, he was homeless in Houston, Texas. He was not always that.

We grew up through the fifties, with Howdy Doody and Sky King, the Hardy Boys, Eisenhower, duck-and-cover, and the Salk vaccine—a pink dot of medicine on a delicious, crunchy sugar cube. We went to Sunday school and church every week. We went trick-or-treating, hung up our Christmas stockings, and hunted Easter eggs. Lonnie played football; I tried out for cheerleader (and lost, while Lonnie was extremely talented on the football field). He was a Cub Scout and then a Boy Scout; I was a Brownie and then a Girl Scout. He sang; I danced. He drew; I wrote. (He wrote too, but I didn't know it until later.) I got mostly A's; Lonnie got, "You could be such a good student if only you would apply yourself."

We played together, and Lonnie made up the games. I was four and a half years younger but bright enough to help improvise our adventures—detectives, outlaws, or our favorite, Olaf and Fredricka the Viking explorers.

Our family relocated every few years. Dad built a career that gave him an ever-greater capacity to provide for us. We were uprooted with each promotion, and the upward mobility meant that Dad would have to travel more and more, sometimes for two or three weeks at a time. It was terribly hard on all of us, including Dad, but, as he said, it was how he showed us he loved us. This explanation would become troublesome later when, as an adult, I had to disengage love from absenteeism.

When Lonnie was in high school, he, too, disappeared for days at a time, sneaking out of the house to go drink with his pals or meet his girlfriend du jour. He left home for good when he joined the Army—a choice he made when faced with the alternative of juvenile detention. His life and mine, seemingly, diverged entirely.

For most of our adulthood, I saw him once a year. I loved him. I cared about him. I felt connected to him. But we were not, and could not be, close. I missed that. I missed him.

Once he became homeless, it was all but impossible for me to know Lonnie on a steady basis. Phone calls, letters, emails—all the ways people now keep in touch—were not readily available to us. So, we communicated through our mother, who had lived in Houston since 1966 and whose phone number Lonnie knew by heart. As long as he was sober and civilized when he called, she enjoyed hearing from him. Mom and I were in touch steadily no matter where I lived, so Lonnie relied on her to pass along his updates.

More often than not, that information was a mixture of fact and fiction. My brother reinvented his reality daily, hourly. Homelessness and alcoholism had damaged his mental clarity; his ability to separate what happened yesterday from what happened thirty years ago was unreliable. Reality, dreams, memories, and invention blurred into the life he reported to Mom. Still, factual or not, the updates confirmed that Lonnie was alive and sufficiently functional to place the phone call.

We got together every Christmas. It was the only time I could be fairly certain I would get to see Lonnie, so I traveled to Mom's house from wherever I lived to be there for the holiday. For him, the one-day visit to Mom's "homestead" was his window onto another life—his only open window, other than his patchy memories.

In the years after Dad died, Mom and I preserved Christmas in a time freeze. The stockings were hung and filled. Angie, the worn Christmas angel who is as old as I am, perched on top of the Christmas tree. The Christmas dinner menu might change slightly from year to year, but the dishes and silver and tablecloth were the same (our grandmother's). The sameness was comforting to all three of us. It tied us to the family we once were as our history peeked out from the Christmas tree branches. Maybe that's why the idea for this book was born on Christmas Day.

The logistics of the holiday went like this: Lonnie usually called Mom a day or two before Christmas, but occasionally on Christmas Eve. Mom handed off the call to me, and Lonnie and I decided where and when I would pick him up. On Christmas morning, I drove to his neighborhood and met him, often (but not always) in the agreed-upon location. One or two of his street buddies waited with him, and I liked to take whoever showed up to breakfast at the local Jack-in-the-Box. Lonnie's friends felt like they knew me because, they said, "He brags on you all the time." They called me "Reverend," sometimes "Doctor." (Lonnie had remade me, too. I have a graduate degree from seminary, but I am not ordained or a reverend, or a doctor of anything.) They never asked me for money, but they always helped me get Lonnie into my car.

I drove Lonnie to Mom's house, and we had our day—stockings, Christmas dinner, mock-fighting over the pumpkin pie, opening presents (Lonnie always brought some sort of gift for each of us), snacking, chatting. At around 7:30 or 8:00 in the evening, we packed Lonnie's loot into a black plastic lawn-and-leaf bag and drove him back to his neighborhood. One year, we decided he could spend the night at Mom's house—a mistake, we later realized, when he had a seizure from alcohol withdrawal, and we found ourselves following a screaming ambulance across Houston to the Veterans Hospital.

The best part of Christmas Day was always the chatting, and it was during one of those chats that this book began. Lonnie was in the backyard, sitting in Mom's rickety wooden glider-swing, having a smoke. I joined him for some intimate sibling conversation. Without planning to, I launched into a series of questions about his life. "Where do you sleep?" "How do you get food?" "How do you bathe?"

Listening to him talk, I rediscovered how bright and warm he was and had always been. His smile, toothless but unreserved, came from his depths, and his laugh was boisterous and hearty. He laughed as though it felt good, really good, like a big stretch first thing in the morning. He was eager to answer anything I asked, and he was frank and specific. He relished being listened to, though he told me he couldn't imagine why anyone would be interested in him or what he had to say. That grabbed me. Christmas Day was running out, and I wanted more.

So, we figured out a way to continue the conversation for the next four years. I would write questions on the backs of postcards, address them to myself, and then mail them in batches to Lonnie in care of the flower shop on his corner. (That florist made our correspondence and this book possible.) Lonnie would find a pen, write his answer on each card, and throw the card in a mailbox. The postcards would form the core of the book, which would tell his story in his words, with me as tour guide.

Lonnie welcomed the prospect of a joint brother-and-sister project. So did I.

From that initial conception—a first-person report on what it's like to live on the street—this book evolved. It became clear that a book about Lonnie's life was necessarily a book about my life, too. The harder I tried to act as an objective "tour guide," the further from Lonnie's truth I seemed to drift. So, I started over.

In this book, my voice is my voice, and Lonnie's is Lonnie's. I've provided some context where specific facts are missing. But the finished book is a genuine collaboration between Lonnie and me, spanning years and miles, and, because Lonnie died several years before I finished writing this book, spanning life and death.

I received 94 postcards from Lonnie; they are all here. They have different handwriting styles and thick, labored pencil lettering. Some he completed while starkly sober, others when he was drunk to the point of incoherence, or hungover and fogged in. His creativity bumps into his manipulative skill. His compassion collides with his violence. Mean/generous, playful/angry, artistic/vulgar, childish/cynical—it's all right there in the cards. The challenge for me was to live up to Lonnie's standards of honesty.

My brother and I simply continue our chat in Mom's yard swing. Anyone who wants to listen in is welcome.

JAN 23 1994

LISA, REFRIED BEANS!

YOU & YOUR WILD IDEA'S SOUND NUTS (BUT WONDERFUL)!

THERE IS A WORD FOR YOUR "STUFF" (WHICH IS ASTRONOMICLE)!

UNFORTUNITLY I'M EATING REFRIED BEANS WRIGGETT NOW ♡♥

YOU ARE MORE CONSCIENCIOUS (SP)

WHAT YOU LIKE ABOUT ME IS PROBABLY MY FANCY & IGNORANT INDEPENDENCE!

NEVER GROW UP

I love you

P.S. PLEASE LETS DO THE BOOK!

1

February/March 1994

I sent the first package of postcards in a small backpack along with several ballpoint pens (their ink wouldn't run in the rain) and a couple of steno pads, Lonnie's preferred paper for writing. I mailed them to the florist's shop (the one where, as he notes on his first postcard, he did yard work from 10 to 11). In exchange for using the shop's address for his mail, Lonnie helped maintain the small yard and garden around the building. It was located on what I still think of as "Lonnie's corner," the intersection of Westheimer and Montrose in Houston.

WHAT DID YOU DO TODAY, FROM THE TIME YOU GOT
UP TO NOW?
   2:00 AM. TOLD TO LEAVE THE ALL NIGHT
        LAUNDROMAT BY H.P.D.
   3:00 AM STARTED WASHING DISHES
        & OTHER CHORES AT THE TWO PESOS
        MEXICAN RESTAURANT
   6:30-7 AM - RELAXED, SMOKED, AND WAITED
        FOR MY CHRONICLES.
   7:00-10:AM SOLD PAPERS ON THE MEDIAN.
        DID OK.
   10-11 DID YD. WORK AT THE FLORIST'S
        SHOP ACROSS THE ST.
   11-2 WENT TO SLEEP. (CAT NAP)
   2:00 GOT MY BAG (YEAH!!) AND
        WROTE MY FINE SISTER ORGANIZED IT
                              LOVE LONNIE

Card 1

The laundromat was about a block away from Lonnie's corner. With a dozen or so industrial dryers running, it was nice and toasty, a luxury suite where Lonnie could sleep stretched out on a bench or snuggled into a corner. But patrons were apt to become alarmed at the sight of him, imagining him unconscious from drugs or alcohol, armed, crazy, or dead. The police often received indignant calls to come and clear the place out. Lonnie might not have appreciated the disruption, but he always had a Plan B, and a Plan C. He was resourceful.

Plan B was a casual Mexican restaurant called Two Pesos, handily situated on another side of Lonnie's corner. It had an outdoor seating area where Lonnie could eat and linger as long as he didn't pester the paying customers. The servers, mostly young women, slipped Lonnie food, placing it in the dumpster out back, carefully wrapped and suitable for warming in the microwave at the nearby convenience store. "You have to know who puts it in the dumpster," he says on the card. Sometimes he paid them back by sweeping up at closing time.

From a very early age, Lonnie had a way with the ladies. He had blueberry eyes, dark hair and, at least as a youngster, a smile full of perfect teeth. In junior high and right into high school, he never wanted for girlfriends. Even at his most street-tattered, he had charisma.

WHAT DO YOU DO IF YOU'RE FLAT BROKE AND YOU NEED A LITTLE $ FOR FOOD OR CIGARETTES, ETC.? HA! 1st OF ALL THE MONEY IS NOT IT. I'TS THE THINGS IT BUYS! – FOR INSTANCE; pg. CHEESEBURGERS – MEX. FOOD – ITALIAN – USA – Ect. ARE ALL FRESHLY PUT OUT AT BREAK – LUNCH – DINNER. YOU HAVE TO KNOW WHO PUTS IT IN THE DUMPSTER AND THEY WILL PUT ENOUGH IN A BAG THAT YOU CAN MICROWAVE AND EAT AS WELL AS THE CUSTOMERS. (PG) AS FOR CIGS? JUST PICK UP A BUTT + SOMEONE WILL GIVE YOU ONE! P.S. THE MICROWAVE IS FROM THE STORE THAT TAKES YOUR MONEY.

Card 2

Besides his barter-style jobs at the flower shop and Two Pesos, Lonnie had actual employment selling the *Houston Chronicle* on the median strip somewhere along Montrose Boulevard. He said it was the job he held longer than any other job he had had. He enjoyed the work, being out in the fresh air at dawn, and chatting with his "regulars." "They look for me," he told me in a letter. "I like that." He had fans.

He had always found ways to have fans. He formed at least three or four different rock and roll bands when he was in high school. I remember two of them: The Beach Nuts and The Rising Sons. I was an enthusiastic groupie, feeling a tide of coolness wash over me because I was related to that cool guy playing guitar up on stage. Mom went to hear his bands play, too, and so did Dad when he was in town. Lonnie also had fans who watched him play football, and Dad was at the front of that line, with the cheerleaders close behind. Lonnie dated the girls who hollered his name the loudest.

The *Chronicle* job suited him. It was also the job that eventually put him in a wheelchair, when a driver in a hurry jumped the curb, bounced onto the median, hit Lonnie at almost full speed, and drove off. The injuries landed Lonnie in intensive care; when he left the hospital, he was able to walk, but only with a cane. Either the repair to his leg was not complete, or the healing did not progress perfectly—maybe both. Neurological damage made the left leg weak, almost spastic, and over time (and in his unhealthy living conditions), it deteriorated until Lonnie finally had to remain in a wheelchair to avoid constantly falling over.

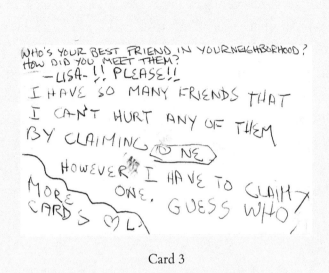

WHO'S YOUR BEST FRIEND IN YOUR NEIGHBORHOOD?
HOW DID YOU MEET THEM?
    —LISA-!! PLEASE!!
I HAVE SO MANY FRIENDS THAT
I CAN'T HURT ANY OF THEM
BY CLAIMING ONE
    HOWEVER I HAVE TO CLAIM
MORE   ONE. GUESS WHO?
CARDS ♡L

Card 3

Lonnie had a lot of friends—they often joined him on Christmas morning when he was waiting for me to pick him up. None of them ever asked me for anything, and eventually I figured out that they didn't have an agenda. They were friendly to me, but respectful, and whoever was available was always quick to help me load Lonnie and his wheelchair into my car.

I asked Lonnie about a "best friend" because there were a few names he mentioned fairly frequently. Each one had a street name, which were the only names I ever heard Lonnie use: Granny, Papa Smurf, Montana (that turned out to be his real name). Lonnie had a street name, too: Fatboy, a tribute to the beer gut he sported as a result of his addiction to alcohol. In later years, he was no longer fat, but he was probably the oldest guy in his neighborhood, and he got a new name: Pops. Violence, malnutrition and unrelieved dirtiness reduce life expectancy on the street, making a gray-haired old guy a rarity.

Lonnie was at the center of a large social circle even in elementary school. His teachers were sure he could be an excellent student if only he would "apply himself" to schoolwork as readily as he did to making friends. For Lonnie, making friends was effortless. He was generous, funny, bold, creative—all his life, people were drawn to him, sometimes in spite of themselves. This card reminds me of that little boy who had many friends but couldn't possibly choose just one to be his best.

When he said "I have to claim one. Guess who," I'm pretty sure he meant me.

Card 4

Lonnie started drawing cartoon figures like this in junior high. As a teenager, he created a character named "Urgl" (I can't vouch for the spelling) who appears in a few of the later postcards. Lonnie's artistic abilities extended to painting and sculpture, musical composition and lyric writing. He had very little training in any of these, none at all in music, other than whatever he picked up from singing in children's choirs and watching Mom play piano. His talents inhabit every postcard. This goofy hero-dog was the subject of some of Lonnie's best tales. Soc (short for Socrates) the Mog (I'm not sure what a mog is—maybe it's Soc trying to pronounce "dog" around his snaggled fangs) was friendly but "took no crap off of anybody," as Lonnie once told me. Soc chased police officers who bothered Lonnie. He fetched Lonnie's belongings from wherever they were stashed. He sniffed out good meals in the dumpsters. Soc was an affable, if ugly, mutt—a gritty blend of bulldog, terrier, pit bull, and maybe a little pig mixed in. "Good morning," Soc says courteously, "Walk me?" Lonnie and I toyed with writing a children's book about Soc, but I'm not sure Soc's stated philosophy would translate well. He was the perfect companion for Lonnie, though. Smart, loyal, fearless, philosophical. With his unruly teeth and off-brand looks, only someone with superior perception could see and value Soc's finer qualities.

I got some of that musical ability, picking up guitar easily after Lonnie taught me my first four chords. I tinkered with piano lessons but didn't learn how to read music very well. Like Lonnie, if I played a piece once or twice, I could play it by ear without looking at the music. I got bored with the kind of simple pieces you learn at first, but couldn't graduate to more complex pieces because I couldn't read the music. I stuck with guitar until I could play almost any song more or less adequately. Lonnie and I played and sang together occasionally at Christmastime. Our whole family was musical to one degree or another, but Lonnie seemed to breathe it the same way I breathed writing.

I had none of Lonnie's artistic ability. I once took a kindly night course called "You, Too Can Draw." Turned out I couldn't. Lonnie was the artistic one; I was the schoolish one. But we each laid claim to our fair share of music.

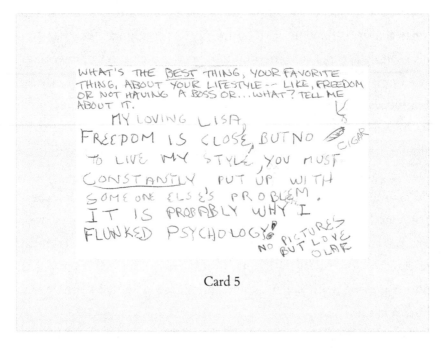

WHAT'S THE BEST THING, YOUR FAVORITE THING, ABOUT YOUR LIFESTYLE -- LIKE, FREEDOM OR NOT HAVING A BOSS OR...WHAT? TELL ME ABOUT IT.

MY LOVING LISA,
FREEDOM IS CLOSE, BUT NO CIGAR TO LIVE MY STYLE, YOU MUST CONSTANTLY PUT UP WITH SOMEONE ELSE'S PROBLEM. IT IS PROBABLY WHY I FLUNKED PSYCHOLOGY.
NO PICTURES? BUT LOVE OLAF

Card 5

Oh, how I wanted an answer! This was the first of several cards on which, in a variety of ways, I asked the question that lives in my heart still: Why? I was working full-time, with a boss and responsibilities and taxes and car payments, and from where I sat, Lonnie's life offered, if nothing else, freedom from all that. I made my best guess, but it was from my perspective, not Lonnie's.

His response is uncharacteristically negative. "Someone else's problem" may have meant another street person looking for drugs or money, a police officer swinging a nightstick, or a store owner who didn't want Lonnie on the front step. His answer only prompted several later questions about how he coped with all the frustrations and irritations. What answer did I want? Was it, "Yes, freedom, it's wonderful, and that's why I chose this lifestyle, and I am well satisfied with my choice." Or did I *really* want, "You know what? There's nothing good about my lifestyle. Help me find a job and an apartment, will you? I've had enough." I couldn't imagine that he actually might be content and at peace with his lifestyle and with himself. Even if I had believed that, I'm not sure it would have been enough for me. I think I wanted him to have not necessarily my lifestyle, but one that would accommodate my need to have a steady, close relationship with him. I wanted him to want that, too.

As for "I flunked psychology," this is fiction: Lonnie never took any course in psychology. He earned a GED in his 20s but didn't go to college.

He signs his name "Olaf" on this card. Olaf was a Viking explorer, a powerful, swashbuckling man who feared nothing, a hero among his people. His partner in exploration was a courageous young woman, Fredricka, who was Olaf's tireless friend and "second"—in duels, in monster-slaying, even in steering their massive ship through the meanest of seas. Lonnie imagined these people.

When Lonnie and I played together as young children, he was the one who made up the stories, characters and settings. I was bright and could play along, but Lonnie could invent something from nothing. Sharing imagined worlds that were owned and operated by my beloved big brother was exciting and safe at the same time. I was the little sister, but I was learning how to imagine away all limits.

ON ONE CARD, YOU SAID YOU HAVE TO "PUT UP
WITH OTHER PEOPLE'S PROBLEMS," WHAT DO
YOU MEAN? WHAT KINDS OF PROBLEMS?

I PROBABLY SHOULDN'T SOUND LIKE A
GRUMP ABOUT IT. THE YOUNG, NAIVE, ST.
PEOPLE ARE ALWAYS IN TROUBLE. SOME
HAVE BLACK EYES. SOME ARE PREGNANT.
MANY HAVE AIDS. LOTS OF RACIAL HATE.
    I REALLY SORT OF PRIDE MYSELF
AS BEING A ST. PEOPLE'S COUNSELOR.
    ALSO, SOME HATE ME FOR THAT, AND
I SOMETIMES GET HIT & HAVE TO FIGHT.
IF YOU TURN THE OTHER CHEEK OUT
HERE, PEOPLE WILL CONSIDER YOU
WEAK, THAT'S WHAT I MEANT ♡ LMJ

Card 6

The Covenant House, a shelter for homeless young people, is located just a couple of blocks from Lonnie's corner. Its residents and its walk-in clients are younger than 18 and are at risk from drugs, AIDS, pimps, and every other hazard of the street.

Lonnie no doubt saw himself in some of them and thought he could help them. His message was "Look at me—this is how you'll end up if you don't change your life." But he also gave them information he thought they needed. He clued them in to sleeping at the laundromat. He advised them to spend any money they had on white socks. He cared about them, and they looked up to him, or at least they respected his experience enough to listen to him. Respect was a rare pleasure for him.

The soft heart that made him care about those kids could put him at considerable risk. "I sometimes get hit and have to fight," he said, "If you turn the other cheek out here people will consider you weak."

He fought more than he lets on here. His arms and head bore dozens of scars, many of them acquired in the process of not looking weak.

> Do you EVER GET FED UP WITH THE AGGRAVATIONS YOU HAVE TO DEAL WITH? WHEN YOU GET TIRED OF IT, WHAT DO YOU DO?
> I DISAPPEAR FREQUENTLY. BUS FARE IS 85¢ ~~BUT~~ SELFISHLY I WANT PEOPLE TO MISS ME! (SICK) WHEN I COME BACK THE PEOPLE OR SITUATIONS HAVE TAKEN CARE OF THEMSELVES AND I GET TREATED WITH ALOT MORE RESPECT AND AFFECTION. THE OTHER DAY I HITCH HIKED TO LAKE LIVINGSTON & BACK. WHEN I GOT BACK — NO PROBLEM WHEN I GET AWAY I'M USUALLY FRUSTRATED WHEN I GET BACK I'M USUALLY ELATED.

Card 7

It's the old "You'll miss me when I'm gone" trick. From the five-year-old who runs away from home, all the while watching over his shoulder to see if Mom or Daddy is coming after him, to the husband and wife who bludgeon each other with the threat of divorce—who hasn't tried this tactic when someone got on their nerves?

I have to admit, this card made Lonnie's life sound pretty appealing. Lake Livingston is about an hour north of town, far enough to feel completely separated from whatever is left behind in Houston. Of course, with all the financial obligations that come from having a home and owning a car—rent, electric bills, car payments, insurance—I could not afford to disappear from my job and give my boss time to miss me. But coming back to "a lot more respect"—that sounded awfully good.

There is casual wisdom in this strategy. He characterizes the desire to be missed as "sick," but walking away from situations he couldn't (or chose not to) control allowed them to "take care of themselves."

When Lonnie writes in rhyme as he did at the end of this card (frustrated/elated), I suspect he was toying with an idea for a song lyric. Maybe rhyming was his way of adding a writerly embellishment. Or maybe he was just playing.

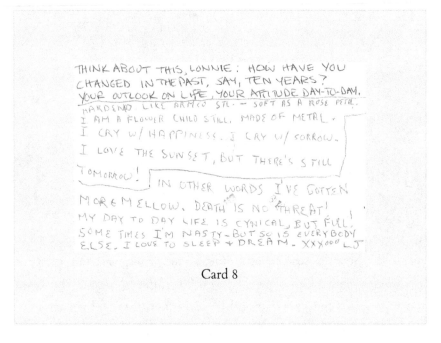

Card 8

Here is another song lyric, with rhyme and meter, ready to be set to music. Lonnie sounds dreamy (and says as much at the end of the card), but his handwriting is straight and sober. I agreed with his characterization of himself—hardened, but soft as a rose petal.

The first image in Lonnie's lyric (or poem)—being "hardened like Armco stl [steel]" — is related to our father. Dad worked at Armco Steel Company for much of his career, starting with the company in the 1940s as a steel mill worker. With persistence and intelligence (and driven by a desire to provide well for his family), he moved into industrial engineering and rose through a series of higher (and better-paying) positions. The price was that the travel demands increased with each new job. We lived in Topeka, Kansas, when Lonnie was in high school and I was in junior high. At that point, Dad was gone for three weeks at a time, home for a week or two, then off on the next trip. He called home frequently, sent us postcards, and brought us surprises from exotic-sounding places like Mangum, Oklahoma.

But the absences were hard on everybody, just as the relocations were. Until we finally settled in Houston in 1966, we moved every two or three years, creating brutal disruptions in our lives. Mom and Dad always presented moving as an exciting adventure, assuring us that the new friends we would make in our new home would be just as good as the ones we were leaving behind. Lonnie's charm got him through those moves pretty handily, enabling him to, as Mom called it, "squat fast" and settle in with a new group. With each move, I held more tightly to what anchored me: making good grades in school. As Dad was absent more and more of the time, Lonnie strayed further and further from home's center, and from me. I clung all the closer to Mom. She was the one who was always there, always available, always reliable. Lonnie came to count on her sturdiness, too.

When Dad was home, he was 100 percent with us. He loved to be around his family. He loved to pile everybody into the car and go for a drive. He loved intensely and without reservation. But then he would leave again. "Dad has to travel for work—he works awfully hard because he loves us." So, we learned, love and leaving were a natural pairing.

When Lonnie said on this card, "Death is no threat," he did not mean that death was not constantly at his shoulder. Many street people carry weapons of one kind or another—one aspect of the homeless-person stereotype that is based in reality. Because Lonnie lived in survival mode, he adapted to the reality of violence. His cane served as protection; he also carried a knife and had ferocious fist-fighting skills. But he could adjust his perception to provide himself with a reality that suited him better. He knew better than to let his guard down, but he got so used to having it up that it felt comfortable and natural. As he wrote, "My day to day life is cynical but full."

"I love to sleep and dream." Sleeping and dreaming were a reliable respite from intense boredom and oppressive surroundings. Drinking and passing out provided another.

WHAT'S THE BEST PLACE TO SLEEP IF YOU GET CHASED OUT OF THE LAUNDROMAT? TELL ME ABOUT A COUPLE OF PLACES YOU LIKE AND WHY YOU LIKE THEM.
FUNNY YOU SHOULD ASK. LAST NIGHT THE LAUNDROMAT WAS RAIDED. THE BEST PLACE TO GO IS A FINE OLD ABANDONED HOUSE. THERE ARE SEVERAL WITH COVERED FRONT PORCHES TO KEEP OFF THE RAIN. THEY HAVE TO BE BOARDED UP, AND THEY HAVE TO BE AWAY FROM ST. LIGHTS. (HAUNTED HOUSE? YOU BET. I JUST STAY CLOSE TO MY CANE, LISTEN TO THE RAIN + SLEEP LIKE A BABY. THE OTHER CHOICE IS JAIL. SPEND THE NIGHT EAT, PLEAD GUILTY, OUT BY NOON. ♥ LMJ

Card 9

"Raided" suggests a planned police operation; the truth was probably a call to the police from a laundromat patron who felt threatened. Unless summoned, the police rarely bothered with homeless people. Being rousted made hardly a ripple in Lonnie's nights; in fact, apart from the inconvenience of having to haul his stuff to another spot, the relocation often felt like an improvement. He once showed me some of the abandoned houses in the neighborhood where he could sneak in and "sleep like a baby." Every city has them; they attract homeless people as well as an assortment of other, less benign types. Eventually the city decides to get rid of urban blight, meaning both the buildings and the squatters, and tears the rickety structures down. But in the meantime, they offer people like Lonnie a warm, dry place to spend a night.

Lonnie was perfectly comfortable with the idea of sleeping in a "haunted house" ("You bet," he says, "I just stay close to my cane"). Even a haunted house was better than the other choice.

"The other choice is jail," he says, but it was an option he didn't prefer. It was simple enough: "three hots and a cot." It afforded indoor accommodations, something Lonnie avoided unless intolerable weather (or rampaging mosquitoes) demanded a retreat. The county provided medical care, which was useful if Lonnie had a seizure from alcohol withdrawal once he was in the cell. It came down to the cot and the meals, both luxuries that were not part of Lonnie's day-to-day life. He didn't especially value them, and even toward the end of his life, he still said he preferred to sleep outside, under the stars, as long as someone didn't steal his cane, or his backpack, or his wheelchair.

HOW DID YOU MEET GLORIA? | OH BOY!
HARLEY JOHNNY + ZOT CAME TO MY APT.
WHEN I WAS WORKING AT ___ CINEMA.
SHE WAS BOTH INDEPENDENT + ALOOF. SHE
STROLLED AROUND THE APT. WITH HER RED HAIR
+ BRIGHT BLUE EYES, LOOKING AT EVERYTHING I
HAD ON THE WALLS (ORIG. ART ECT.) AND WENT TO
THE BATHROOM. ZOT, JOHNNY + I WERE TALKING
ABOUT HER + GETTING DRUNK. SHE WAS GO-
ING W/ JOHNNY. I SAID "GOD SHE'S BEAUTIFUL"
JOHNNY SAID "YOU CAN HAVE HER. THAT GOT ME
P.O.ED. SHE CAME OUT FROM THE BATH ROOM +
INTRODUCED HERSELF. I SLOWLY STOLE HER.

Card 10

Lonnie in love!

When he met Gloria, he was working for a friend of Dad's who provided an apartment and a job for Lonnie. When Dad died of cancer in 1988, Dad's friend took Lonnie under his wing, setting only one condition: Lonnie had to stay sober. Not one to be comfortable under anybody's wing, much less under anybody's authority, Lonnie came to resent being a ward, and the arrangement lasted only a few months. As he notes on this card, he, Zot and Johnny were getting drunk.

Gloria was his last serious girlfriend. Lonnie had been married twice—both ended in divorce. He makes it clear that when he met Gloria, he was smitten. "Oh boy!" he says as he starts his recollection, and "Love at first sight," he wrote on the back of the card.

She was independent and aloof, with red hair and blue eyes. She strolled around the apartment looking at his artworks. How could he not be captured by a beautiful woman who appreciated his art?

Johnny's disrespectful comment triggered Lonnie's chivalrous instincts. He said he "slowly stole her," but I doubt it took very long. She was in his life for a long time, until he found out she was married. They remained friends until she died a year or two before Lonnie's death.

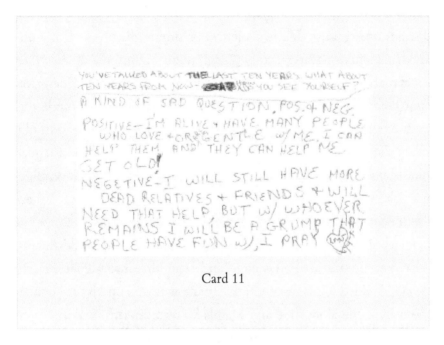

Card 11

I wasn't sure I wanted to ask Lonnie this question. He rarely focused his attention beyond his next meal or beer or place to sleep. Besides, I had no trouble conjuring visions of Lonnie's future, and none of them were much to look at. But I had asked him to look back, and now I wanted him to look ahead. I was curious whether he would even have a forward view, and whether his forward view would resemble what I imagined was ahead for him.

It didn't. After Dad died, Mom and I were on the front line of Lonnie's hazardous life. While we constantly braced ourselves for the worst — the phone call from the police or the hospital — Lonnie worked his interior magic on his future as he did on his present. His positive view is what anyone would want to see in their future "many people who love and/or are gentle with me," and people who can help each other get old. He does allow for a pessimistic view, but it is only one option, and even that option ends well, with him an old grump "that people have fun with."

Lonnie had plenty of dead friends. People on the street died of diseases or exposure, fell to violence, or simply disappeared. Lonnie also had plenty of dead relatives. Our Dad died in his mid 60s in 1988, a loss that devastated both of us. Our grandparents on both sides, two aunts and an uncle had died. But the loss that clung to Lonnie the most bitterly was his daughter, Abigail Dawn. She was three years old when she drowned in the bathtub. At the time, Lonnie and Magda, the baby's mother, were divorced, and Magda was in a relationship with the man who later would become her second husband. When Lonnie wrote this postcard, Dawn had been dead for nearly 20 years.

It has always been tempting to say that his daughter's death was what put Lonnie over the edge and sent him into alcoholism. It certainly added to his momentum. But he was well on his way before the baby came along. He and Magda were musicians, making their living in the rock music world, where alcohol, drugs and recklessness surrounded them constantly. Lonnie's freefall accelerated, while Magda found her way, somehow, to a safer and saner path.

WHEN YOU USE THE TERM "STREET PERSON," WHAT
DOES IT MEAN TO YOU? 1ST. PEOPLE ARE
LIKE THE SONG BY CHER "GYPSIS
TRAMPS & THIEVES" HOWEVER, STREET
PEOPLE ALSO INCLUDE RUINED LOVE,
DOWN TRODDEN, YOUTH, UNWANTED
PREG., AND HONEST PEOPLE WHO
ARE JUST CONFUSED, LONELY, OR
BOTH. THEY ARE IN THE PURSUIT OF
LIFE, LIBERTY & THE PURSUIT, OF ?
HAPPINESS. (FAMILIAR)

Card 12

Cher's song came out in 1971, and it referred to the labels used by the "people of the town," who presumably looked down their noses at the "gypsies, tramps and thieves." As he goes on to explain, Lonnie didn't deny these labels, but he knew they were not the whole story of street people. "Ruined love, downtrodden, youth, unwanted pregnancies, and honest [double underlined] people who are just confused, lonely, or both."

Where did he see himself in that catalogue? Maybe he meant to describe himself with the next phrase: "In pursuit of life, liberty and the pursuit of happiness." Earlier, on Card #5, Lonnie pointed to the people around him as an impediment to freedom, as the source of problems that had to be put up with. As he wrote that card, he clearly didn't feel a sense of freedom. On Card #12, written just over a week later, he speaks of these same people with compassion and empathy. But he refers to "they," not "we."

Surprise, challenge, adventure—that's Olaf talking! "Now," he writes, "it is wisdome and responsibility (my own)." At age 47, Lonnie was seeing himself as a wise old man, and, relative to life expectancy on the street, he was probably right. He was wise in the ways of the street, and he had responsibility for himself (and, pointedly, *only* for himself).

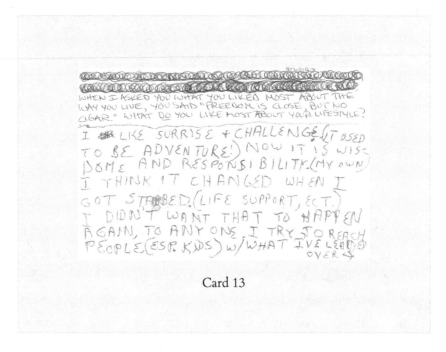

Card 13

Lonnie had always said he never wanted to grow up, so to take responsibility for anything was a major change of perspective. The event that Lonnie believed precipitated that change was his closest brush with death (other than seizures that occurred whenever he was in alcohol withdrawal). It happened when he was stabbed by another street person. He had multiple wounds; one nicked his liver, another collapsed one of his lungs, and yet another missed his heart by no more than half an inch.

He told the story this way: He was asleep (passed out drunk) in an entrance to a business in his neighborhood. Another man, an acquaintance of Lonnie's, was similarly passed out in another doorway nearby. An owner called in a complaint against one of them and a police officer came to shoo them away. Adhering to standard police procedure, the responding officer applied a kick or a tap with a nightstick to the sole of Lonnie's foot. This roused Lonnie right away, but when the officer tried it on the other man, it failed to get through. Seeing the problem, Lonnie helpfully stepped in and shook the man by the shoulders. The man came up swinging, a knife in each fist. He punched Lonnie repeatedly in the chest and abdomen, blade-first, until the policeman pulled them apart and called an ambulance.

Lonnie was taken to Ben Taub Hospital, where he was admitted immediately to the intensive care unit and placed on a breathing machine (the "life support" Lonnie referred to). He was in intensive care for nearly two weeks and then moved to a regular room for another two weeks before he was discharged.

He didn't want that to happen again to anyone, he wrote, and he started to try to reach kids with what he had learned, "sometimes to my expense," he added on the back of the card. This life-altering experience had made him realize that he could help other people avoid similar disasters. What was the expense to him? Maybe some people were less receptive to his advice than others, and maybe the less receptive ones expressed their displeasure violently. He alluded to that on Card #6. "I pride myself as being a street people's counselor," he said. "Some hate me for that, and I sometimes get hit and *have* to fight."

Did you make A DECISION TO LIVE "ON THE STREET"
OR DID IT JUST EVOLVE THAT WAY? FIRST IT
EVOLVED. I HAD SO MUCH FUN LEARNING
WHAT GOES^(ON) OUT HERE, THEN WHEN
I HAD LEARNED ENOUGH, I JUST DECIDED
TO USE EVERYTHING THAT ABSORBED.
(IN SCHOOL, THE ARMY, BY GOOD & BAD
EXPERIENCES) LYRICS + MUSIC WERE
MY MAIN WEAPON. THEN CAME
PAWPS PHYSICAL THING (POWERFUL BUT
GENTLE) THEN IT BECAME A KIND
OF "ROBIN HOOD" DECISION, BECAME REAL! (THEN IT & LAST)

Card 14

This card is puzzling.

It was another of my attempts to get an explanation—something I could grab that would make Lonnie's life make sense to me. He says here that he had fun learning what goes on. I don't know how he learned that without being on the street. When he had learned enough, he says, he just decided to use everything he had absorbed in school, the Army, by good and bad experiences. Use it for what? Use it by living on the street, I suppose he meant, but in the end, everything he had learned left him homeless, penniless and powerless.

"Lyrics & music were my main weapon." Weapon against what? Was it his main weapon against losing himself entirely? He was a skilled musician, especially for someone who had no training, but he never quite made a sustainable profession of it. Who was his audience? How were his listeners affected by his music and lyrics, by his condition and his appearance?

"Pawp's physical thing"—"Pawp" was Lonnie's name for our father.

The physical thing he's referring to, I think, is Dad's diagnosis with terminal cancer in 1986. But there was nothing gentle about the road it took Dad down. "Powerful" it was—it disassembled my world and, I think, Lonnie's even more.

He and Dad were alike in many ways, a fact that may have hampered their relationship more than it helped. Dad was highly self-disciplined and orderly, but he also had a healthy streak of "test the limits." Often the limits he tested were his own. For example, when he lost his job at Armco Steel in 1968, he joined the Texas National Guard (at age 44) and proceeded to go through both airborne training and jumpmaster school. My mother was horrified, if reluctantly impressed; even his instructors ribbed him about being too old. But the inappropriateness of the decision was a large part of its appeal. At first glance, joining the military looked like the ultimate "establishment" move, but after a long business career and at his age, it was both startling and baffling. He had something to prove, to himself of course, and some 35 jumps later he was finally satisfied with the proof. Dad was tough, physically and mentally, and could survive and thrive in the harshest of circumstances. And there it is—the aspect of street life that may have proven Lonnie to himself.

The last comment, "a kind of 'Robin Hood' decision," stumps me. I followed up on later cards (Chapter 3, Cards 29 and 30), but Lonnie's answers on those cards were not very helpful. Of course it is a heroic image. But he was not stealing from anybody or giving to anybody in the "Robin Hood" sense. It may have been simply a roguish image that appealed to him, and, as he said on Card 30, a romantic one. I find it striking, though, that he underlined "decision." Living on the street was not something he fell into, or slid into. He wanted to be clear: It was a decision he made.

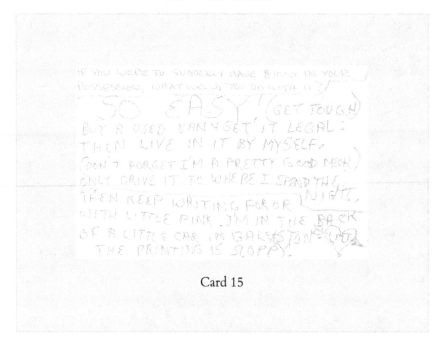

IF YOU WERE TO SUDDENLY HAVE $1000 IN YOUR
POSSESSION, WHAT WOULD YOU DO WITH IT?
SO EASY! (GET TOUGH)
BUY A USED VAN & GET IT LEGAL:
THEN LIVE IN IT BY MYSELF.
(DON'T FORGET I'M A PRETTY GOOD MECH)
ONLY DRIVE IT TO WHERE I SPEND THE
THEN KEEP WRITING FOR OR NIGHT.
WITH LITTLE PINK. I'M IN THE BACK
OF A LITTLE CAR IN GALVESTON & WHY
THE PRINTING IS SLOPPY.

Card 15

"Buy a used van, get it legal, live in it by myself, only drive it to where I spend the night"—this is one of the few places where Lonnie's fantasies are grounded in reality. He *was* a pretty good mechanic. As a teenager, he was an avid student of cars and all the details of their engines and body styles. He taught me about hubcaps—stock, bullet, spinner and moon. I remember being in the back seat of our family car at Allen's Drive-in in Topeka, on our knees, facing out the back window, watching the cars cruise around and identifying the hubcaps on each one. With $1,000 seed money, Lonnie would have had no trouble making this fantasy happen. So many times I've read this card and wished it had.

"Little Pink" is me, as in "little pink angel." It sounds like the kind of name a boy might call his little sister who through most of her childhood seemed incapable of getting into trouble. The truth is, I rarely did. Lonnie had being bad pretty much sewn up, and the role that was left to me was to be the "good little girl." I worked hard in that role. But the problem with it was that I never knew how good was good enough. Lonnie started misbehaving in significant ways when he was in elementary school, so when he did something good, like an "A" in a school subject, it was conspicuous. I got row upon row of them, but lingered at much more length over my rare "B," which I considered inappropriate and dangerous. Misbehavior was not an option for me, and for the same reason: It wasn't in my job description.

Maybe Lonnie felt that delineation as much as I did. It might be called "self-fulfilling prophecy" now, but then it was simply the bad boy being bad and the good girl being good. Writing with me—the postcards for this book, and maybe more—took on added significance. It represented (as it does for me) a merging of the two half-people into one whole, a collaboration between the brother and sister who at some point fell apart from each other. Olaf and Fredricka would stand together again in the bow of their great ship.

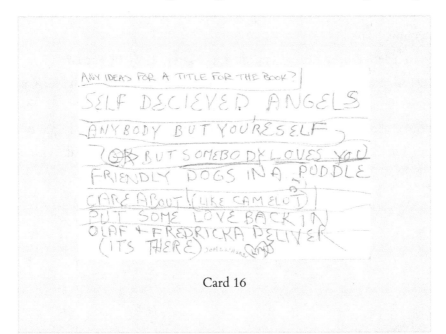

Card 16

The titles Lonnie proposed provide a wide-angle picture of his life on the street and a multifaceted portrait of him. "Self-Deceived Angels" seems out of line with the others, which all revolve around kindness, love or caring. Perhaps that was at the core of the deception: What masqueraded as love and friendship on the street was often pure self-serving manipulation—a con job whose prize might be alcohol or cigarettes, a safe place to sleep, sex, bug spray or other forms of street currency.

"Olaf and Fredricka Deliver" is probably the most straightforward of his titles. For Lonnie and for me, "the book" became an icon. It was a collaboration between us—Olaf and Fredricka back together, alive and well and sharing an adventure. It was also an exercise in restoring, maybe remodeling, a relationship that we both had missed. I suspect it was something more for Lonnie—as much present affirmation as legacy, the book would give form and substance to his chaotic and decidedly formless life. It was a way of grabbing onto what was left to him of reality, at least the reality he most wanted to occupy. "The book" was a way home.

In a letter he wrote to me during March 1994 (it appears in the Introduction at the beginning of this book), he described the idea as "nuts (but wonderful)" and added a post script: "Please let's do the book." The title "Olaf and Fredricka Deliver" is like an epilogue on our childhood adventures, the imaginary Vikings made real, with a book left behind to verify their existence.

WHAT DO YOU DREAM ABOUT?/THIS IS FUNNY
YESTERDAY I WAS IN JAIL FOR
ABUSIVE LANGUAGE. I HAD A TECH.
COLOR DREAM ABOUT HAVING MY
NOSE STAPLED TOGETHER W/ PURPLE
STAPLES, + I WAS STILL LOOKING
CROSS EYED TO CHECK THEM OUT.
(IN COURT?) CASE DISMISSED! I HAVE
BEAUTIFUL DREAMS IN COLOR. TOOKIE
YOU, MOM, + DAD. SOME IN DETAIL
LOVE DOESN'T DIE

Card 17

On an earlier card, when Lonnie said he liked to sleep and dream, it triggered for me a torrent of images of a tortured man who could find peace only in the mock-death of sleep. What a happy surprise to read the first few words of his answer to this question: "This is funny." He reports a dream he had while in jail (probably enjoying an overnight break from heat and mosquitoes). In his description of the dream, the distinction between his real-life court case on the charge of abusive language and the dream about the purple nose staples is blurry.

In his "beautiful dreams," all the people he loved ("Tookie, you, Mom and Dad") were alive and living in Technicolor. "Tookie" was his pet name for his daughter, who drowned when she was three. At the time Lonnie wrote this card, Dad had been dead about eight years. Lonnie dreams about all of his family, "sometimes in detail." He closed with the statement, "Love doesn't die." He knew he was loved by those four people, all the people to whom he was related by blood.

In his dreams, he had all the love he needed, enough to last until the next dream.

Had he recalled the verse in the Bible, "Love never ends" (1 Corinthians 13:8)? It certainly is a well-known verse, at the end of a passage that is read at virtually every wedding and at least half of all funerals. Lonnie went to the same churches and Sunday schools as I did, until he left home at age 17. Maybe that verse stuck, and resonated when he needed it.

Or maybe he was simply making an observation.

WHERE DO YOU GO TO JUST CLEAN UP?
    USUALLY ONE OF MY FRIEND'S
PLACES, BUT NEVER TWICE IN A ROW.
SOMETIMES I HAVE TO GO TO A
SHELTER — TAKE A SHOWER — GET THE HELL
OUT OF THERE. I HATE SHELTERS...
TOO MANY LAZY BUTTHOLES.
    OTHERWISE I CARRY A BAR OF
IVORY SOAP — GO INTO A RESTROOM.
(FILLING STATIONS ECT) + TAKE WHAT
IS COMMONLY CALLED "A WHORE BATH!

Card 18

This is one of the few cards where the coarse, hard side of Lonnie and his life are visible. His language is more "street," and the specifics he gives banish any romantic ideas of a carefree, unburdened life without responsibilities. I think I asked logistics questions like this because I needed a reminder of the reality Lonnie actually lived. His life took place between meals and showers and bathroom visits, all of which were a struggle. He had no responsibilities, but also no bathroom. He could not impose on friends for two consecutive showers (friends?), he could not stand the shelters, and the best he could get from a filling station bathroom was a "whore bath."

On the Christmases when Lonnie came to Mom's house, he often seized the opportunity to take a shower, and to have Mom wash his clothes while he slept stretched out and wrapped in towels on her couch. (Mom made sure the clothes went through the longest possible cycle, giving Lonnie maximum sleeping time and the clothes the best chance of coming out clean and sanitary.) He also made a point of using the toilet just before we took him back to Montrose, where his options were to try to find a business where the employees would let him use the facilities, or to use the nearest tree and risk being arrested for pubic urination.

I marveled that Lonnie would have the nerve to call people at the shelters—people in essentially the same circumstances as his—"lazy buttholes." But he didn't see their circumstances as equal to his own. "They" were in the shelters because they were too lazy to do anything else, whereas Lonnie was there as a last resort, having chosen the life he was leading and being at the shelter only because he had run out of eligible friends on his shower list. He was self-sufficient, as a rule; they were lazy and dependent. Lonnie made a clear and, to him, highly significant distinction.

The cards for this month were, on the whole, pretty lucid, and perceptibly literate, even literary in places. In the next months, that will happen less frequently. Lonnie's handwriting will be more erratic, his thoughts more jumbled. He will sound more pessimistic, more cynical. But there will be glimpses of the lucid, witty, charismatic writer of these first cards.

2

April 1994

Lonnie sometimes talked about Jesus as though he had sat with him at the bus stop and made friends. Jesus was a street person, a hippie, Lonnie once said. The pictures of Jesus that Lonnie and I grew up with—the long, soft hair, eyes that were gentle, almost dreamy, the mustache and beard—certainly supported that image.

IS THERE ANYTHING YOU MISS ABOUT THE "STANDARD"
AMERICAN LIFESTYLE - A HOME, A CAR, STABILITY....?

NO! I MISS A SPRITUAL THING THAT I
MAY NEVER HAVE AGAIN. I'VE NEVER
HAD STABILITY. CARS ARE FUN.
A HOME? I DON'T WANT! HOWEVER,
THERE IS A WHOLE LOT OF ARMY/HIPPIE
THAT SOMEHOW, KEEPS ME TOGETHER,
I PRAY THIS DOESN'T DEPPRESS YOU,

P.S. IF I JUST HAD A KID- ♡ LJ

Card 19

We went to church as a family throughout our childhood. The hymns we sang are so deeply ingrained in my memory that I can hardly separate them from the safe, solid feeling of sitting in the pew with my family week after week. Although much later I studied and embraced the theology of those early sermons and hymns, as a child I understood clearly the sureness of my family, and that is the sensation I came to associate with being in God's presence. When Lonnie says, "a spiritual thing that I may never have again," he may be talking about that sense of connection, of being safely tucked into something—a family, God's love, a church congregation.

He held my pastor status in high regard, and he was often eager to hear about my experiences as a pastor. During one hospital visit near the end of his life, I acted as pastor to him, serving him Holy Communion in his hospital room. Mom, Lonnie, and I took the sacrament together—the first time we had shared it in several years, and the last time. I read from the traditional Methodist liturgy, Lonnie reciting bits of the prayers right along with me. When it was time for the Lord's Prayer, we held hands and spoke the familiar words together, and with our eyes closed, I imagined we were back in one of the church pews where our family had sat together every Sunday of our young lives. On the day Lonnie wrote this postcard, perhaps he was feeling especially far away from those pews. Yet, after saying that he "misses a spiritual thing," Lonnie ended this card with a prayer for me. Maybe he had more of a spiritual thing than he realized.

When Lonnie says he "never had stability," he may be thinking of all the times we moved. Lonnie lived in five different houses before he was in high school. While I sank rapidly into the sensation of security I found in each new church pew, maybe Lonnie felt homesick for the pews in our previous church. Maybe all those moves are why he could state so emphatically on this card that he did not want a home. (He did admit, however, that "cars are fun.")

The postscript on this card sounds off-handed: "If I just had a kid." More likely, this longing was never far from his consciousness. When I found out that Lonnie's three-year-old daughter had died, I was going to college in New York, and in the middle of final exams. I couldn't get to Houston for the funeral. I was not there when the horror, anger, and bewilderment played out. I was not there to mourn with Lonnie. I don't know how he coped with the pain and grief. It is clear that it never went away, no matter how deeply Lonnie immersed himself in alcohol and denial.

He enjoyed children's company, and they loved him, too. Lonnie savored the image of himself playing Santa Claus at a children's home. He described little ones who crawled up into his lap and whispered their wishes to him, all of them playful and loving and in no danger of drowning in a bathtub. I don't know at what children's home this Santa scene took place, or even if there ever was such a scene. It was real enough for Lonnie, and just describing it put a genuine and heartfelt twinkle in his eye.

Lonnie was a doting father to Tookie, and for that matter, Dad was a doting grandfather. (In fact, Tookie and her grandpa had such an affinity for each other that the rest of us often had to beg for a turn at holding her or playing with her.) Lonnie especially enjoyed rolling around with her on the floor, tussling and tickling, and she repeated a sequence of giggling, escaping, and then hurling herself back onto him for more. They were like a couple of puppies. Lonnie swore he would never grow up; of course, he would connect easily with children. And of course, he would miss them. There were not many children on Lonnie's corner.

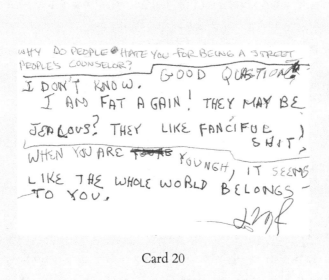

Card 20

The sprawling, inconsistent letters and the broken thoughts on this card suggest that Lonnie was either drunk or hung-over when he was writing it. Four-letter words are a surprisingly rare occurrence throughout the cards. Maybe thinking about why people resent him made him angry and the obscenity just popped out.

He made a reference to being "fat again." At times he had a large beer gut, a common sight among street people whose main source of nutrients may be beer or wine. At other times, however, such as when he was in the hospital with an injury or illness, he went through enforced detox and ended up with no appetite, losing a lot of weight very quickly. His street name, "Fatboy," never changed, though, until he came to be seen as an elder and people started calling him "Pops."

"They like fanciful shit. When you are youngh, it seems like the whole world belongs to you." Lonnie may have sensed that the young people he "counseled" didn't want to hear his reality-based story. They preferred to believe that they were living the good life of freedom and self-expression—"fanciful shit." Lonnie's perspective may have been unpalatable, but it was certainly authentic. He remembered a time when he felt like the world belonged to him, but he lived daily with the reality: It didn't.

Whenever I was with Lonnie, I struggled with one central question: Does he want it this way, or is he in total denial? He seemed not to notice how bad his living conditions were—having to scavenge for meals, cigarettes, clothes, a place to urinate without getting arrested. From the perspective of my life of comparative comfort—job, apartment, car, friends, church—his life looked un-survivable. But he rarely complained or indicated in any way that he wanted out of it, until very late in his life, long after he wrote these cards.

"I'm going to record an album and make a million." This was Lonnie's fanciful mantra for most of his life. He had the talent to back it up; what he lacked was the capacity to do the work required. He recoiled from responsibility of any kind, and that included showing up for the meetings, rehearsals, recording sessions, and contract signings that dominate an artist's time. So, without the attention from professional arrangers, producers, and managers that results in million-dollar albums, the many songs he wrote languished. I don't know that his songs were of that caliber—I am the starry-eyed little sister, after all—but he never gave his "fanciful shit" a chance to be anything else.

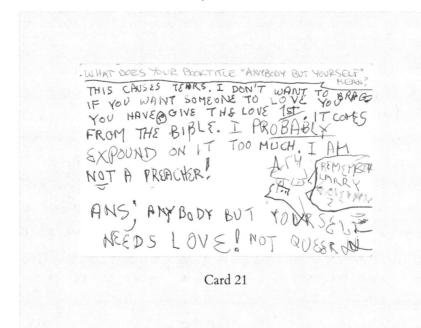

Card 21

Lonnie was a fairly easy crier. He bore his emotions near the surface, especially if he had been drinking. Clearly the subject of love—loving or being loved—was painful for him. He had lost, or removed himself from, the people who loved him most. He may have had friends on the street, but they were not the loving kind. He was divorced from two wives, and he had lost his little daughter. He was out of touch with Mom for weeks at a time, and his contact with me, although frequent during the postcard-writing periods, was otherwise limited to Christmas day. The cards were a lifeline for him. In addition to giving him a sense of purpose, they enabled him to stay connected to me. He knew I loved him.

I see the Sunday School influence, of course. He's right that the idea of loving others comes from the Bible (among other sacred texts), but he has it a little bent. In his version, loving others is a way of getting them to love you. He may not have meant it that way here, but it would be in keeping with the barter-based culture of the street, and with his ability to manipulate people into meeting his needs.

Even as a little boy, Lonnie was intent on making people love him. His teachers bemoaned it on his report cards; now, he might be described as "highly socialized." He made friends easily but alienated them just as easily by testing the limits of their tolerance for his bad behavior. He tried smoking, drinking, shoplifting, and other boys-will-be-boys missteps, urging his friends to go along. Those who passed the tests stayed around. If Lonnie was not the instigator—if someone else was testing his limits—he went along happily, often raising the ante by embellishing the offense. One drink became two, one cigarette became a pack, then buying a pack, or, even better, stealing one.

Lonnie made a point of specifying that the love he was referring to was "not queer." With prostitution in all forms fairly common on the street, it is possible Lonnie had recently been approached by another male offering an encounter. Such an offer would have made Lonnie angry, especially if the propositioner was very young. His use of the word "queer" was not unusual for the street, but in the 1990s, it was a derogatory term. Lonnie wasn't homophobic, but the particular brand of homosexuality he encountered on the street had little to do with loving, committed relationships. It had everything to do with expediency, self-preservation, and exploitation. Indeed, the street brand of any relationship was rarely much more than that.

The sketch at the right side of the card is "Urgl," the character Lonnie created sometime in junior high. Urgl was deformed and often had large teeth, but he was a generally friendly character, and Lonnie sometimes used Urgl as his own signature. In this sketch, Urgl mentions a boy whom Mom recalled as a friend of Lonnie's, an all-American boy, good student, well-behaved, handsome. His memory seems to have floated more or less randomly to the surface of Lonnie's awareness. Maybe he remembers this friend fondly, or maybe with a shadow of remembered jealousy.

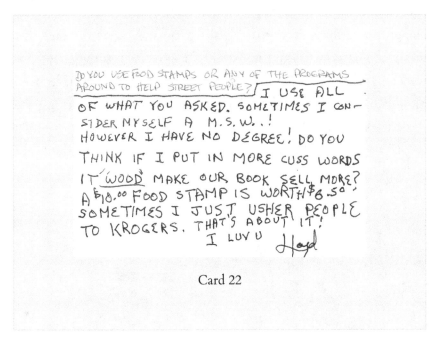

Card 22

When Lonnie says he used food stamps, he is not talking about going to the appropriate government office, filling out the paperwork, and having them issued. There were plenty of people around his corner who preferred to have cash in hand to buy the things food stamps couldn't—alcohol, cigarettes, drugs. He points out that a $10 food stamp was worth $6.50. He could buy one and get more food for his money, or he could convert one to cash if he wanted something to drink or smoke. Or, he could "just usher people to Kroger's." I can imagine him chatting them up as he accompanied them to the door, charming them into handing him a little cash. On his best days, when he was sober and in a sunny mood, he was hard to resist.

Where does the crude question about putting more cuss words in the book come from? Someone nearby may have said something to him that brought it to mind. Or, like the memory of his classmate on the previous card, maybe it randomly floated up into his consciousness. Whatever prompted it, he didn't see it as an inappropriate thing to say to his sister; or, maybe he did and that was precisely why he said it. He might have been showing off for someone who was reading over his shoulder. It would have been more like him simply to be snickering as he imagined shocking the "little pink angel." He returns to his sunny self when he signs off, "I luv u," and he signs his name formally, "Lloyd." This is the only card he signs that way.

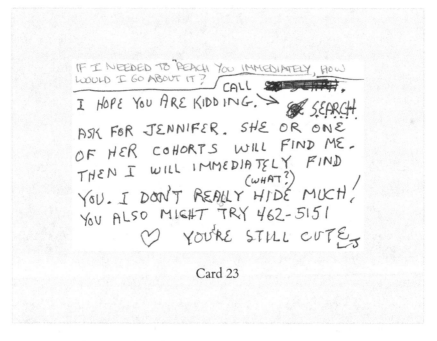

IF I NEEDED TO REACH YOU IMMEDIATELY, HOW WOULD I GO ABOUT IT? CALL ~~████~~. I HOPE YOU ARE KIDDING. → SEARCH. ASK FOR JENNIFER. SHE OR ONE OF HER COHORTS WILL FIND ME. THEN I WILL IMMEDIATELY FIND (WHAT?) YOU. I DON'T REALLY HIDE MUCH! YOU ALSO MIGHT TRY 462-5151 ♡ YOU'RE STILL CUTE

Card 23

As our mother aged, I often thought about how I would let Lonnie know if she were in the hospital (or worse). I had had mixed results with trying to find him by searching around his neighborhood. I occasionally visited Houston for a few days at some time other than

Christmas, and during some of those visits, I might decide to try to see him. With no way to let him know I was in town, much less to make arrangements like we did at Christmas, I'd drive to his corner and start looking. How hard could it be, I thought. He didn't range far from that intersection, and I knew his preferred hangouts from years of Christmas rendezvous points—the Kroger parking lot, the convenience store, the gas station, the laundromat.

But street people are incredibly good at disappearing themselves. This is a skill Lonnie developed as a defense against the police. If, for example, he needed to sleep off a binge, he hunkered down in a spot where he would be invisible from the street and could count on several hours of uninterrupted napping.

This propensity for hiding (despite his denial of it on this card) was only one reason why I could ride up and down Westheimer or Montrose for hours and never spot him. Other reasons: He could be in jail. He could be in the VA hospital, or Ben Taub, the charity hospital. On a cold, rainy day, he could be wrapped in a blanket on some beneficent person's front porch. I successfully hunted him only once in all the times I tried.

SEARCH is a Houston organization that provides services for homeless men, women, and children, with an emphasis on helping clients find jobs and, ultimately, get off the street. The group also gives people food and clothing—Lonnie was this kind of client, turning to SEARCH when he needed immediate, short-term help. He probably made an impression, though, flirting with Jennifer, easily making friends with her and her "cohorts."

I've met another such friend of Lonnie's, a young woman who worked at the Covenant House near Lonnie's corner. He had mentioned her to me, so I went to meet her and ask what she could tell me about him. Her memories were specific and unambiguously fond. She referred to him as precious, charming, with a beautiful smile. She especially recalled his bright blue eyes. She no doubt saw him relating to the young people in her care. I can imagine the first time she saw him in the yard, chatting with one or two teenagers, making them laugh, sharing a smoke. She might have crept up to eavesdrop, concerned for the wellbeing of her charges. But she would have seen him at his very best.

> YOUR CHOICE! HOW! / IT'S AROUND 8:00 AM. EVERY ONE OF MY EARLY MORNING ST. PEOPLE ARE AS DRUNK AS SHSHEAKSPEAR. I DON'T UNDERSTAND. MY PARDNER THAT I'VE WORKED W/FOR 3 YRS. IS SINGING SONGS! I'M TICKLED, I'VE BEEN THRU THE CARDS. ONLY ①IS HARD! YOU ARE A KITTEN! love from me, LJ

Card 24

It's startling to encounter Lonnie when he is the only sober person in the scene! His handwriting on this and the previous card is clear and fairly consistent, and his spelling and punctuation are reasonably good. He is writing after getting up near dawn to sell the *Houston Chronicle* on the median with his "pardner" and is puzzled to find that everyone around him is "drunk as Shakespeare." He's tickled, I think, by the funny and ironic scene—himself, sober, gazing around at a bunch of drunk people while a friend sings songs. It's easy to be tickled along with him.

I enjoyed the insight into the procedure he followed when he received the packets of cards from me. He looked through all the cards before starting to write anything, maybe shuffling the order, thinking about his answers. He rated each card hard or easy, and only then began to compose his replies. On several cards he asked me to be tougher; on this one, he seems to have appreciated the light touch. Before signing off, he calls me a kitten—cute, like on the last card, and harmless.

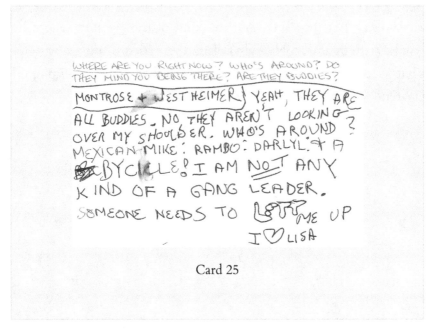

WHERE ARE YOU RIGHT NOW? WHO'S AROUND? DO THEY MIND YOU BEING THERE? ARE THEY BUDDIES?

MONTROSE + WESTHEIMER) YEAH, THEY ARE ALL BUDDIES. NO THEY AREN'T LOOKING OVER MY SHOULDER. WHO'S AROUND? MEXICAN MIKE. RAMBO. DARLYL. & A BYCICLLE! I AM NOT ANY KIND OF A GANG LEADER. SOMEONE NEEDS TO LET ME UP I ♡ LISA

Card 25

I wanted to know what it was like for Lonnie to just hang out. I wondered whether he was ever allowed to sit somewhere and smoke a cigarette or just feed the pigeons without someone calling the police (not that I would have done differently if I were a business owner thinking of my customers or finding some homeless guy lounging around on my property). He's on his corner, Montrose and Westheimer, and a few buddies are nearby. Apparently, Darlyl is new to the corner, since he doesn't have a nickname yet. I never met Mexican Mike, but I did meet Rambo and, true to his name, he was wearing the signature bandana tied around his head, Stallone-style.

In their company, Lonnie was keeping the cards to himself. He said they were not looking over his shoulder, buddies or not. Keeping something private on the street was not easy. There was no way to lock something up, or to hurriedly secret something away in a drawer when someone approached. Rambo and the others were the kind of friends who could be counted on to give Lonnie a light (and maybe a cigarette), but they were not the kind of friends with whom he would share the cards. He didn't claim these friends, and he was not a gang leader. He didn't invite them any further in than the tip of his cigarette. The cards were between Olaf and Fredricka.

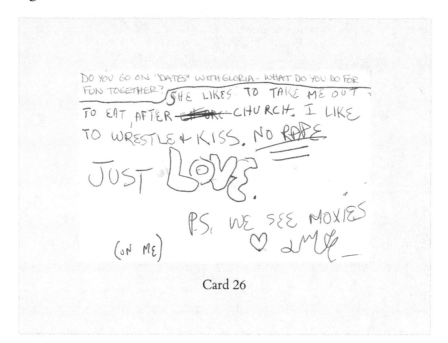

Card 26

If not for the jarring disclaimer, "No rape, just love," this card would sound like any romantically involved couple. Lonnie and Gloria went to church and out to eat afterward. They did a bit of wrestling and kissing, went to movies. He declares "no rape," separating himself from that dark aspect of life on the street. Women are especially at risk, as sex could get them food, drugs, alcohol, or a warm place to sleep for a night. But often, young women and men who resist cajoling or seduction might be drugged or simply overpowered, often by members of gangs. That may be one reason why on the previous card Lonnie denied so vehemently being a "gang leader."

Lonnie was in love with Gloria, and she with him. I saw them together only once, but I saw that they followed each other around the room with their eyes, like any two smitten people would. Gloria liked to take him out to lunch, but, he noted, when they went to see movies, it was on him. I wish I knew what movies they saw, and whether he liked popcorn as much as I do.

Card 27

The "your choice" cards were a way to get a glimpse of what might be on Lonnie's mind at any given moment. I wondered what was important to him, what issues he spent time thinking about, what worried him. On this card, unsurprisingly, his daughter was on his mind. His pleasure at having his choice of how to use the space on the card led him to say I was his "favorite chick ever." (That still makes me smile.) He trusted me. He knew he could put anything on the card, and I would be happy to have it. So, he drew.

The figure on this card is one that I saw elsewhere in Lonnie's artwork—a female with long, black hair. She usually is seen from the back, and she is often nude, as she appears to be here. Because this is labeled with his daughter's name, the nudity is innocent, and she leans against a wide, welcoming tree in a peaceful, natural setting. The object in her hand looks oddly like a gun, and the position of her arm—outstretched as though she were taking aim—contributes to that impression. But Lonnie would not associate that action with his daughter, and in fact, he had no interest in guns. More likely the object was meant to be a book, or a bird.

He fairly shouts his signature—"MORE CARDS PLEASE"—and sends me a big heart and a cluster of kisses and hugs.

Card 28

Because I told Lonnie that the next card was not for the book but just for him and me, I am not presenting it. But I will note that what I asked him was whether he had any questions about my life. I suddenly felt like I was carrying on a relationship with him that resembled that of a doctor or therapist: I was hearing all about him, he was hearing very little about me. I thought I should make it clear that he was welcome to poke around in my head, too. I think I wanted to make the relationship seem more reciprocal, more equal. But the truth is, in this dialogue, I was the asker, Lonnie was the answerer. He was entirely comfortable in his role; in fact, he obviously relished being invited to express himself, and, even more, knowing someone was paying attention to what he said.

He did ask a question: "Do you feel like you are mistreated?" I don't know what prompted him to ask this. I was working full-time in an ad agency, a demanding job but one I enjoyed, and I was about a year beyond the last of my chemotherapy treatments for breast cancer. I was also considering ministry, seminary, and what to do when I grew up. If anything, it was one of the most vibrant periods in my life.

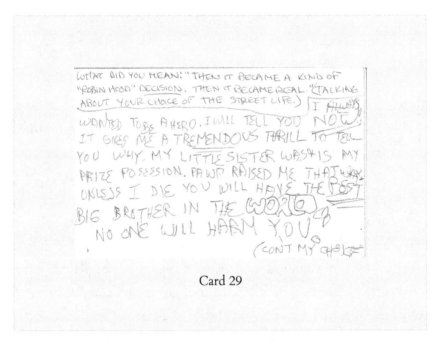

Card 29

I suppose that, from Lonnie's perspective, my life looked complicated and vexing; it surely would have been impossible for him to imagine himself living it. Maybe this question was simply his way of making sure I was okay.

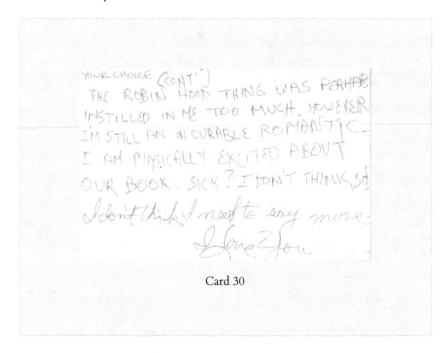

YOUR CHOICE (CONT')
THE ROBIN HOOD THING WAS PERHAPS
INSTILLED IN ME TOO MUCH, HOWEVER
IM STILL AN INCURABLE ROMANTIC-
I AM PHYSICALLY EXCITED ABOUT
OUR BOOK, SICK? I DON'T THINK SO
I don't think I need to say more.
Love You

Card 30

My question here referred to Card 14. When Lonnie talked about a "Robin Hood" decision, I could guess what he meant: Robin Hood was a bigger-than-life figure in the same genre as Olaf and Fredricka—brave, free, self-sufficient, and adventurous. Lonnie had one word for all that: hero.

There is, of course, a part of me that has always been very much the starry-eyed little sister. When Lonnie was in rock-and-roll bands as a teenager, I was always front and center at any gigs they played, most often parties hosted by our church youth group or dances at the local recreation center. I never missed his football games or track meets. When he went away to the Army, I wrote his service number all over my notebook. I remember the number to this day.

Not that our relationship growing up was without conflict. He could be too rough, and occasionally even mean. I remember one time when he and a couple of his friends—all in about fourth or fifth grade—invited me to play "fort" with them. I was eager and unsuspecting. They coaxed me into imitating our Dad's silly make-believe laugh, "har-de-har-har," and then nudged me toward mispronouncing it so that I was saying "hor-de-hor-hor." They laughed hysterically and, thinking that I was regaling them with my comedic imitation, I kept on saying it. Mom finally intervened when she could hear them roaring all the way inside the house. I didn't figure out the joke until years later.

There were many more occasions when Lonnie was the "best big brother in the world," including those afternoons spent exploring on a Viking ship, or engaging in swordplay in Spain. He taught me how to imagine. Later, when I was in high school, he taught me how to play guitar. One of the best dates I ever had was many years later, when a boyfriend took me to a club where Lonnie was performing. Lonnie invited me onto the stage to sing and play with him. I have no idea how good or bad we were—both of us had drunk a few beers—but the experience of making music with my brother was dreamlike. He had always said he was going to "cut a record and make a million," and I thought it was entirely possible. But that night, I was in that fantasy with him. We were Olaf and Fredricka the rock stars.

On Card 30, Lonnie described himself as "an incurable romantic." It was true of him on so many levels—he was sentimental and deeply emotional, and he lived in his imagined world of good guys and bad guys, never ambivalent as to which he was.

He said he was "physically excited about our book." He noticed how that sounded, even to him, and confidently dispatched the uneasiness by asking, "Sick?" and answering, "I don't think so." He had revved himself up, finally vowing to be the "best big brother in the world." Suddenly, the prospect of doing the book with me, whom he loved with the intensity of an "incurable romantic," was so pleasurable that he had to express it in the most impactful terms he could find. Maybe he even wanted to be shocking about it, emphatic in the extreme.

His handwriting changes abruptly and dramatically for the next sentence: "I don't think I need to say more." Different mood; he's reined himself in, satisfied that he has made his point. Just to be sure, he signs, "I love you." Message(s) received.

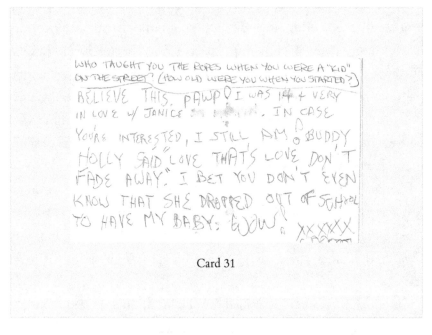

Card 31

The question of when Lonnie first found himself living on the street is one he never answered—I doubt he knew. On an earlier card, he said it evolved, and I believe that's about as accurate a description as he could give. On this card, he says he started at 14. He doesn't mean he started on the street at age 14. When Lonnie was 14, our family had just moved to Topeka, Kansas, from Atlanta, Georgia. Lonnie was entering ninth grade, which was the end of junior high in Kansas at that time.

As an athlete, even in a brand-new school, he was a great success. He was a member of the football and track teams and demonstrated talent and passion for both. The desire to continue to qualify for the sports teams forced him to maintain a passing grade average; if not for sports, he would have had little interest in school subjects. Sports were how Lonnie acclimated to his new environment, and they gave him entree to the highest social circles of junior high. The girl he refers to was cute and popular, a natural partner to the quarterback on the football team.

I'm sure Lonnie was in love with the girl and, as his hormones rioted, he must have wanted to try out manhood. I'm fairly sure he didn't get her pregnant, nor did she leave junior high to have his baby. However, it is believable that, even at age 47, he remembered what it was like to be in love with her. The rest may reflect his earlier sigh: If I just had a kid. Maybe, he could imagine, he was Daddy to his junior high sweetheart's kid.

Lonnie's relationship with our parents was particularly tumultuous during this period. The move to Topeka had landed Dad in a job that paid better but demanded that he travel much more than he ever had before. He was out of town more frequently and for longer periods, leaving Mom to try to handle a growing and increasingly troubled teenaged son. While I clung ferociously to being good—in school, Girl Scouts, church, Sunday school, even overachieving at summer day camp—Lonnie ventured further into misbehavior. He drank with his friends, whose parents had well-stocked liquor cabinets, as most adults did in the Dean Martin 60s. He smoked when he could get cigarettes. Our parents smoked, so that was not much of a challenge; hiding the smell was a bigger challenge.

And he ran away. His bedroom was in the corner of the basement, widely separated from the rest of our rooms upstairs. It was common, and a good idea, for teenagers to have their own bedrooms. This afforded them some privacy while still keeping them accessible to vigilant parents; it also accommodated listening to loud music without deafening the rest of the family. But it did something else for Lonnie: It gave him almost total freedom at night.

In Kansas, houses were built with window wells—basement windows below ground level with a small semi-cylindrical space carved into the ground outside the window so light could get in from above. In Kansas, at the heart of America's "Tornado Alley," all houses had basements, and window wells were an ingenious way to light them. They also afforded Lonnie an ingenious way to escape the basement at night and take off, unheard and unseen, and to return in time to "get up" for school, with the entire adventure undetected. Once Lonnie discovered how to use this private entrance and exit, he could freely disappear for an overnight or a few days.

Our parents were at a loss. More accurately, Mom was at a loss, since she was a single parent whenever Dad traveled. Lonnie knew he could defy any kind of discipline Mom tried to enforce. However, "Wait 'til your father gets home" had significant power. Lonnie and Dad tangled more than once on a physical, man-to-man level, shouting, shoving, sometimes throwing things or knocking over furniture. I don't remember witnessing actual blows, but that may be because by the time their fights approached that point, I had already withdrawn (or been sent) to another room precisely so I would not witness the escalating conflict.

Lonnie may have viewed these confrontations as a form of boot camp that prepared him to be tough on the street when necessary. Dad saw to it that Lonnie participated in Boy Scouts and played football (Lonnie loved football, though, and was good at it). When Lonnie got into enough trouble to risk being kicked out of high school, it was Dad who suggested that a stint in the Army might be just the thing to instill discipline and responsibility. Lonnie was 17 when he enlisted; his experiences in the Army taught him a lot of things, but discipline and responsibility were not among them.

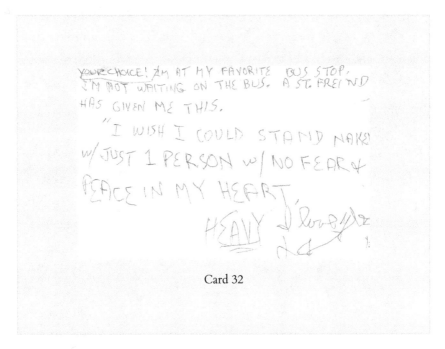

Card 32

Lonnie wrote this card on April 27, the anniversary of the day our dad died. Whether he realized it or not, I can't guess, but if he was aware of the date, he might have had Dad on his mind as he wrote this card. I doubt he had regrets about Dad. He knew he had disappointed Dad numerous times and ways. But Dad, just days before he died, had risen out of semi-consciousness to settle accounts with Lonnie.

Mom, Lonnie, and I were in the room with Dad, whose morphine drip was making him drift rhythmically between incoherent and lucid. As we watched him, his eyes focused, he reached out for

Lonnie's hand and said, "I forgive you." Lonnie thanked him and said, "I love you." Dad said, "I love you too, son."

Lonnie's favorite bus stop, behind the Kroger store next to a large parking lot that was always empty, was the favorite bus stop of a lot of street people. It was out of the traffic flow and relatively unpopulated (by pedestrians and cops). People disembarking the bus could be approached for spare change, and they often had it, having dug change out of their pockets for bus fare. The bus stop was near a Jack-in-the-Box, where there might be a little fresh leftover food in the dumpster, and a few "spots"—dropped coins—under the drive-through window.

Lonnie's friend, who gave him this "heavy" thought, spoke for Lonnie and for a lot of people, on the street or in luxury condos, longing for peace, trust, intimacy, and love.

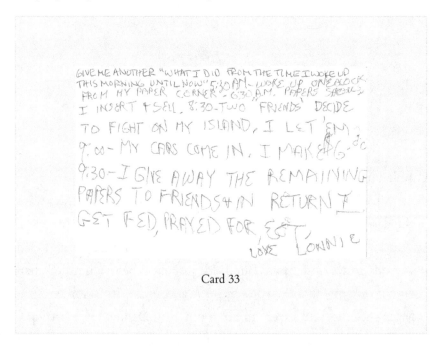

Card 33

Sometimes, even Lonnie knew how to pick his fights. There's no telling what the two friends were fighting about, or if there was a reason at all, beyond alcohol- or drug-induced rowdiness. But Lonnie chose to "let 'em." It was a smart move: He had gotten up early enough to get his newspapers and get situated on the traffic island to sell them. Now his "regulars" were coming along, and by keeping his mind on what he was doing, Lonnie made six dollars.

His next move, giving away the remainder of his papers to friends, was sociable and sensible. It was 9:30 a.m., well past the morning rush hour and any likelihood of selling many more papers. So, he gave them to friends. What else was he going to do with leftover morning newspapers? In return, people gave him food or cigarettes, or prayed for him. Maybe some chatted with him for a few minutes.

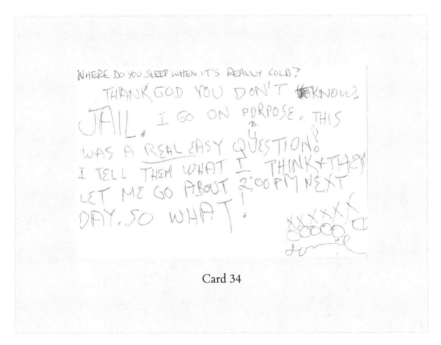

Card 34

There was a hint of normalcy in such transactions; even an opportunity for Lonnie to be generous. He was just as likely to give away the socks we gave him every Christmas, keeping aside just one or two pairs for himself. Lonnie didn't own much, and he didn't seem much interested in having it any other way.

The relative luxuries of Harris County Jail were available anytime Lonnie wanted them. He could call the cops on himself, or, more simply, "tell them what I think." In other words, he could mouth off to the police and they would put him in jail overnight. Lonnie's rap sheet was composed mostly of public drunkenness, disorderly conduct, and other charges that typically led to a brief stay in jail. Of course, stays longer than one night created serious problems—alcohol withdrawal can trigger major seizures. Lonnie often made the trip from Harris County Jail to the VA hospital for further treatment, which usually included a round of the detox program.

Obviously, for Lonnie, the one-night stays in a warm, dry place were a matter of convenience. "So what!" It beat a blanket and a front porch.

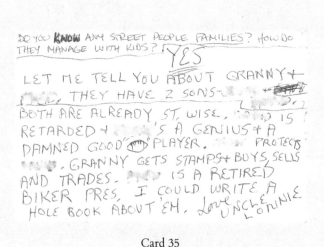

Card 35

I struggled to imagine what it was like for these parents trying to provide school supplies, shoes, and food for their children, let alone safety, security, or simple physical comfort. Lonnie's admiration for this family is evident: a young man who protects his handicapped brother, plays pretty good football, and is already street-wise; a mother who cleverly buys, sells, and trades food stamps, spinning them into enough food to keep her family going; a dad who is a retired biker president—a position Lonnie considered prestigious and enviable. He signed this card "Uncle Lonnie," which, I'm sure, is what the two boys called him, and how he thought of his relationship with the family.

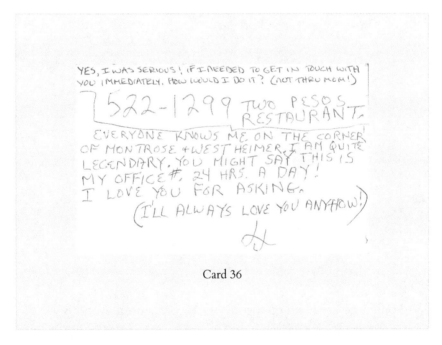

Card 36

This was another try at figuring out workable logistics. This time, Lonnie's answer was probably the most useful he could have given. He was, indeed, known to pretty much everyone on his corner. If I needed to find him, I had only to ask at the gas station, the parking lot behind Kroger, the Two Pesos restaurant or, as a last resort, the police station. If the police knew where he was, he could only be in one of two places—the hospital or jail—and neither of those options was good news, although the hospital at least meant Lonnie was safe, clean, and being cared for. Jail meant that too, more or less, but he was a lot harder to reach in jail than in the hospital.

He said he loved me for asking. If I might need to get in touch with him in a hurry, that meant he was still a member of the family. It made him an insider. It made him mine and Mom's.

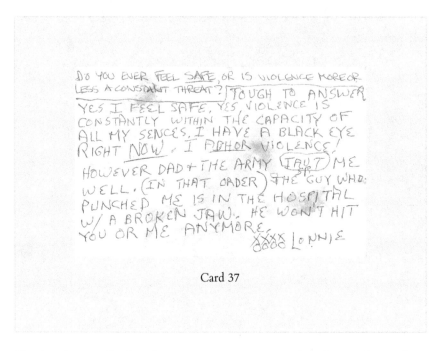

Card 37

I had only one firsthand opportunity to see my brother in his violent mode, and it was several years after the date on this card. I was visiting Mom at her house in Houston. I hadn't been able to let Lonnie know I was going to be in town but, once I arrived, I didn't want my brief visit to be consumed by the complexities and stress of trying to reach him. So, I hadn't tried.

Lonnie happened to call the house, and, thinking I could at least talk to him on the phone, I answered. We chatted for a while, and then Lonnie suggested that I come pick him up in Montrose and bring him out to Mom's house. I knew Mom would not want that. Lonnie was impossible to deal with if he was drunk, and if he stayed sober for too long, he was subject to withdrawal-induced seizures. So, I said no. He wanted to come out to the house. I kept saying no as gently as I could, and he finally backed off and said he loved me, and we ended the call on friendly terms.

About an hour later, there was a knock at the back door. I could see Lonnie through the small window. I knew I couldn't let him in; when I cracked the door to tell him no, sure enough, I smelled alcohol. Luckily, I had left the chain lock on the door. He cursed and threatened to push his way in, and he probably could have torn the chain out of the wall if he had put his weight into it. Instead, he pushed a knife blade through the space. It missed me. The second he withdrew it I slammed the door shut and locked the other two locks; one was a deadbolt. I yelled that I would call the police if he didn't leave, but that I really didn't want to do that. He left.

He called again the next day. He didn't remember what had happened, or at least he said he didn't. I wish I could say I know he wouldn't have hurt me. I know he wouldn't have hurt me if he were sober. But this was the first time I had seen him in a fully out-of-control-drunk condition. I don't know what he was capable of.

He may have sincerely abhorred violence as a matter of personal preference, but it was all around him on the street, as he said on this card. He was rarely without fresh bruises or cuts whenever I saw him, and he was eager most of the time to recount how he had incurred them.

Lonnie said Dad and the Army taught him about violence. I have trouble thinking that Dad purposefully taught Lonnie to be violent, but the physical nature of their confrontations when Lonnie was an older teenager must have communicated on another level. They were both athletic and competitive, and both had hot tempers, although Lonnie's tended to flare quickly while Dad's smoldered before exploding.

The Army's role was in equipping Lonnie for combat—the physical conditioning, hand-to-hand techniques, and general principles along the lines of, "Protect your head and keep a low center of gravity." In survival mode on the street, his temper and his training may have kicked in at about the same time, making him fully capable, psychologically and physically, of breaking some guy's jaw. In the end, though, even that violent action translated, in Lonnie's mind, to a protective action on my behalf—"He won't hit you or me anymore."

TELL ME ABOUT THE CHURCH YOU GO TO W/ GLORIA.
THE NAME OF IT IS CHURCH IN THE CITY
IT IS NONDENOMINATIONAL. THE MUSIC
+ DANCERS TRULY GLORIFY THE LORD.
(HOUSTON BALLET—JESUS ROCK BAND)
EVERYONE PREACHES, BUT THE
ORDAINED ONE IS A FUNNY SAINT
WHO IS STRAIGT LACED BUT DISERVES
LONG HAIR. YOU WOULD LOVE IT.
SERVICES ARE 2 HRS OF GLORY.
NEXT TIME YOU'RE HERE, GO W/ US!
ITS IMPOSSIBLE TO EXPLAIN

Card 38

I never had a chance to go to the Church in the City with Lonnie and Gloria. It sounded exuberant and freewheeling, but I was a little less adventuresome than Lonnie gave me credit for, and I feared feeling like an alien. Lonnie clearly enjoyed the church, and the "funny saint" at its head, and the music was custom fitted for Lonnie. I wonder whether he ever sat in with the band; I'm sure he would have wanted to.

He said "everyone preaches"—I imagine he meant that people gave their spiritual testimonies. It would have been interesting to hear Lonnie tell his story. It would not have followed the typical plot, "I found the Lord and cleaned up my life." Lonnie's story would have been a report not on how Jesus helped him get off the street, but what it was like to live on the streets *with* Jesus.

3

June 1994

What is going on with these next three cards? The language and spelling are not as literate as Lonnie's previous cards, and the handwriting is completely different from his usual scrawl—at first, I suspected someone else had written them.

YOUR CHOICE! All names have been changed to protect the ultimate or the guilty, you ever watch two dog in a puddine weattes There fighting argueing playing or whatever there having fun They play get wet and they shake it off on there masters

Card 39

But the voice is Lonnie's, the personality in the words is Lonnie's. The disconnectedness of these cards is unsettling.

Lonnie was on his corner, shortly after a soaking summer rain, watching two dogs wrestling and nipping at each other, growling and snarling. At first, they seemed to be fighting, really going at it, baring their teeth at each other, and knocking each other over. But then their master called to them. They stopped and looked each other in the eye, tails swinging wide, and, as their master approached, they gave a vigorous nose-to-tail shake, drenching him in water and mud. Lonnie must have laughed out loud. I wonder who Lonnie had in mind for the dousing he would have delivered by shaking off his mud.

These dogs and their puddle are not anchored in time. On Card 16, written in March (three months earlier), Lonnie suggested a title for this book: Friendly Dogs in a Puddle. Events, people, and scenes repeat themselves throughout the cards. Lonnie's conception of time was distorted by a lot of factors; alcoholic blackouts, withdrawal seizures, boredom, the sameness of his days. In fact, the complete non-necessity of keeping the dates straight would have been reason enough to let his memories and himself slip around in time. Lonnie made his present more acceptable, more entertaining, by letting it drift randomly among memory, reality, and imagination.

I was, of course, the beneficiary of the nimble imagination he had even as a kid. It took me to Spain, Hollywood, ancient Norway, and to the deck of a mighty Viking ship on a raging sea. It was like being God, able to move freely along the spectrum of time, tinkering with events and people's lives, even our own. Lonnie was like a dementia patient—lots of memories, clear as slides under a microscope but jumbled together into a patchy, perpetual now.

Mental illness may have been mixed in there, too. When he was in the Army, he defied authority and rules so insistently that he was released on a general discharge (offered as the only credible alternative to the medical discharge recommended by the Army psychiatrist). He was desperately homesick throughout his time in the military, but especially while he was stationed in Germany. It became clear to his superiors that, far from teaching him responsibility as Dad had hoped it would, being in the Army had pushed his misbehavior to its extreme.

He left the military and moved back in with us in Topeka. As soon as possible, he resumed his misadventures. He raided the liquor cabinet. He smoked. He violated his curfew (ignored it, actually). His worst (and last) offense before he entered Menninger Clinic was driving his brand-new Volkswagen "bug" straight down the wrong side of Burnett's Mound. Burnett's Mound was a manmade hill at the top of which sat Topeka's water tank; it had a steep side and a more gradual slope for maintenance access. The area at the top around the tank was a notorious lover's lane, and I'm sure Lonnie had exploited its seclusion and romantic ambience many times. The night he hurtled down the steep side and into the ditch at the bottom, he was drunk and, thankfully, alone. He was not hurt, but that totaled VW was the last car Mom and Dad bought him.

It also served as their last straw. Realizing that they had to do something to try to stop Lonnie's spiral, they urged, pressured, and ultimately convinced him to check himself into the Menninger Clinic in Topeka in 1965. Being voluntarily committed, of course, meant that he could check himself out whenever he wanted, but during the initial weeks of his treatment, he was supposed to stay on campus 24 hours a day, every day.

I am not sure I knew at the time that he was in a mental hospital. Mom has shown me letters he wrote to the family as he made plans to be released from Menninger and, later, to move to Houston where we had relocated. But he didn't reveal the nature of his environment, often simply saying, as he did in phone calls to Mom years later, "Tell my little sister I love her."

At 18 years of age—an immature 18—he coped with the constraints by doing what he did best: He rearranged his reality. He entertained himself by sneaking on and off campus and bringing alcohol onto the grounds. These were small but, for him, empowering infractions. Then he met "Jo" (not her real name) in one of his therapy groups and fell madly in love.

As he was settling into his own agreeable version of life in the mental hospital, Armco announced that Dad was being transferred to Houston, Texas. We would be moving some 700 miles away and leaving Lonnie behind—unless he checked out of the hospital.

Love prevailed. He insisted on staying at Menninger under the legal supervision of our family's lawyer. Then Jo was released. But, lovestruck, she stayed in Topeka, probably near the hospital, and the two continued their relationship.

Jo was 16 years old. When her family, and especially her father, got wind of her now-19-year-old, mental-patient boyfriend, they came to Topeka and reclaimed her, taking her back to Kansas City, an hour away. Naturally, Lonnie found ways to get to Kansas City. Powered mostly by the fun of breaking so many rules, the romance continued for some months, until, inevitably, Lonnie got caught climbing back in over the hospital fence. The lawyer, worn down by the long series of calls from the hospital staff, decided he had had enough. Lonnie was all too willing to check out of the hospital, and by that time the romance with Jo was losing its luster. Lonnie headed for Houston, carrying with him his Army records, his general discharge papers, and a diagnosis of sociopath.

Whatever else they felt at hearing that diagnosis, Mom and Dad must have felt a measure of relief that there was a name for what drove Lonnie to rebel so resolutely against authority, structure, or expectations of any kind. It didn't make him any easier to control or even to live with, but it did, in some measure, explain him.

Sociopathic behavior includes manipulation, lack of empathy, and a lack of regard for socially acceptable behavior. As a child, Lonnie had what in retrospect looks very much like a benign version of these symptoms—he made friends with incredible ease, giving the appearance of a child who, although conspicuously rebellious, was exceptionally well socialized. But as he grew, his powerful charisma evolved into something less benign. The label "sociopath" made it seem manageable.

Looking through the postcards and seeing so many radically different handwriting styles (such as the ones on Cards 39-41), it's easy to wonder about the possibility of multiple personality disorder. His facility for constructing and inhabiting so many different worlds (an ability owned by many, if not most, children) takes on a pathological character when the adult's identity slips among extremes.

Most of the psychologists and therapists who dealt with Lonnie when he lived on the street were those involved with the substance abuse recovery program at the VA hospital. While terms like "anger management" and "self-control" often entered into his diagnoses and treatments, "sociopath" was a term I never heard from the VA doctors. Perhaps it has fallen out of favor since the 60s. Or perhaps alcoholism so thoroughly eclipsed whatever other issues Lonnie had that they were never fully examined.

Maybe he was mentally ill, or maybe he simply had an arsenal of extreme coping behaviors that suited his extreme circumstances.

Either option provides only the illusion of understanding. ("Oh, *now* I get it—he was like that because he was mentally ill." Or, "That's just his way of coping with his terrible circumstances.") Both are incomplete versions of the truth, which is just another way of saying that neither is the truth. Too bad it's not that easy.

DO YOU PREFER TO WRITE DRUNK OR SOBER? (I PREFER SOBER - YOU WRITE MORE AND YOU WRITE BETTER, BLUNT.)

I like writeing when I'm half Drunk, Because I can think about my verbs & nouns without getting overwrought with my Thoughts & concerns

Card 40

I debated whether to ask Lonnie this question because I was afraid it would influence his writing or make him feel like I was criticizing him. But it seemed to me that the cards he wrote when he was sober gave me more information and insight. He expressed himself more clearly—no surprise—and often at greater length.

That he preferred to write when he was half-drunk makes perfect sense—alert enough to string together coherent thoughts, drunk enough to feel relaxed and uninhibited. He describes something else, too: the ability to focus on the writing itself without "getting overwrought" with his thoughts and concerns—the ability, in other words, to write analytically, even objectively. Did he become overwrought when he was writing drunk, or when he was sober? If it happened when he was drunk, then it is easy to understand why alcohol made an effective anesthetic. If he drank just a little, he was relaxed and articulate; a little more and he might be swamped by his thoughts and concerns. But further into the bottle, he would feel nothing and, in time, pass out. It makes me wonder what he experienced when he wrote sober. It makes me wonder whether he *ever* wrote when he was sober.

WHAT THINGS DO YOU KEEP WITH YOU ALL THE TIME (YOUR CANE, YOUR WALLET...?)

No wallet (To easy to Rob) I do carry my V-A card my cane and a comb The most important thing I carry That no one can take from me is my memory (mom's phone # in Houston)

Card 41

Lonnie didn't carry a wallet because it would be too easy to steal. At the time he wrote this card, Lonnie needed a cane all the time for walking, so he might have looked like an easy target. He was strong and, maybe more importantly, had a powerful survival instinct (and the cane, which, if needed, doubled as a weapon). But he also had a bad leg and was 47 years old, and for at least six or seven of those years he had lived on the street. He may not have been as easy-pickings as he looked, but he was no match for younger, stronger, desperate thieves. He knew it.

He did carry his VA card, the only government-issued identification he owned. He sometimes had a bus pass, and once or twice, a library card. But the VA card got him an ambulance ride to the VA hospital, a crucial convenience when he was spending a night in the county jail and had a seizure induced by alcohol withdrawal.

I admit that I snicker a little when he says he carried a comb with him. A few times, when we were at Mom's house for Christmas, I took that comb he carried and tried to work it through his nasty, matted hair. I did this because I couldn't bear to look at it, but he loved having me do it. He never minded if I pulled hard on a tangle—he would sit with his eyes closed and a cat smile on his face as long as I had the patience (and the stomach) to keep on combing. As it turned out, I usually had just about enough patience to comb it all out, smooth it (or braid it), and kiss him on the cheek when I was done.

The most important thing he keeps with him, he says, is the one thing no one can take away—his memory. He knew Mom's phone number and birthday as well as Dad's and mine, and the approximate date when Dad died. He remembered silly songs we made up as very small children. Silly songs were my particular specialty. One of them, nothing more than a string of rhyming nonsense words sung to a tune, had a physical component that always accompanied the singing. I would hold onto his thumb and little finger (one in each fist) and twist his hand back and forth as though his hand were a steering wheel. At the end of the song, I would make a small crashing sound and pull his thumb and little finger in opposite directions. He always let me, he always braced himself for the pull, and he always evinced extreme, agonizing pain, complete with an appropriately contorted face. It made me howl with laughter. Lonnie remembered "The Lop-o-ton Song," all the words, the ritual at the end, and the required facial acrobatics right up until his last days.

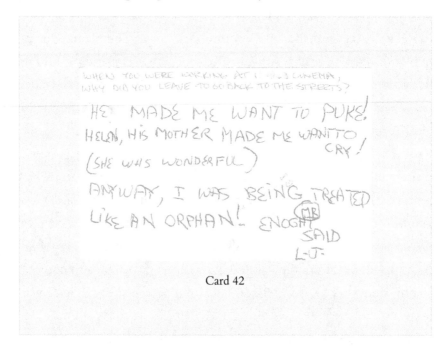

WHEN YOU WERE WORKING AT THE CINEMA,
WHY DID YOU LEAVE TO GO BACK TO THE STREETS?

HE MADE ME WANT TO PUKE!
HELEN, HIS MOTHER MADE ME WANT TO
CRY!
(SHE WAS WONDERFUL)

ANYWAY, I WAS BEING TREATED
LIKE AN ORPHAN! ENOUGH
SAID
L-J-

Card 42

When Dad died, his boss, Dave (not his real name), who was also a close friend, undertook to help Lonnie, I believe as a way of doing something to honor Dad's memory. He hired Lonnie to work for him at his offices, doing general office work, filing, and errands, with a possibility of more if Lonnie showed aptitude and interest. He also settled Lonnie in an apartment and paid the first month's rent, with the understanding that Lonnie would pay the money back over time out of his paychecks. There was one condition on Dave's generosity: Lonnie had to show up sober for work.

Maybe Lonnie enjoyed having the apartment at first. He may have enjoyed the work itself. He'd obviously hit it off with Dave's mother, who worked in the office with him. The whole arrangement required little of Lonnie except his cooperation and the one thing he was all but incapable of doing: Obeying the rule. I don't know whether he was an alcoholic at the time, but even if he wasn't, alcohol obviously played a significant emotional role. I think it became significant for him the moment Dave said he couldn't have it anymore. "Oh yeah?" Lonnie must have thought, "I can have it if I want it." At that point, the issue stopped being whether he could have it and became how he would sneak it. On Card 10, he mentioned that Harley Johnny and Zot were getting drunk at his apartment. At the very least, alcohol was available. I can hardly imagine Lonnie's friends getting drunk while he watched placidly and stayed sober. As always, Lonnie rebelled. With only one rule to break, he took dead aim and broke it.

There was something else, though, that he seems to have resented even more than the rule: the fatherly role Dave took on. "I was being treated like an orphan," Lonnie said, which would have stung Lonnie deeply. Whatever conflict there was between Lonnie and Dad, after Dad died, Lonnie worked his magic on the relationship, transforming it in his memory into one of close compatibility and mutual understanding. I believe they were more alike than either realized, but there was never much compatibility, and even less understanding. The love between them, however, was never in doubt.

For Dave, then, to give any hint of taking on the fatherly role—discipline, authority, guidance, advice, any of it—clearly infuriated Lonnie. It made him "want to puke." The arrangement lasted no more than a couple of months: Lonnie drank, didn't show up for work, and Dave fired him.

I sort of understand the wanting-to-puke thing. Years after Dad died, Mom remarried—a nice enough fellow. Their relationship was cordial at first, but the deeper they got into it, the more they managed to grate on each other. I liked him okay, but I never had the slightest conception of him as a stepdad. Had he acted toward me the way Lonnie felt Dave acted toward him, it might have made me want to puke, too. Our Dad was a big, intense figure in our lives. As far as we were concerned, nobody could touch him.

Dave was not the only person who, over the years, tried to help Lonnie get off the street. Various charities, the VA, Mom and I, and even some of Lonnie's friends took a shot. He valued his freedom, or what passed for freedom in his perception, too much to be constrained by work, rent, schedules, or sobriety. It went deeper than that, I think. He didn't see his life as something he wanted or needed to be liberated from. He was less than unwilling or uninterested. He was unaware.

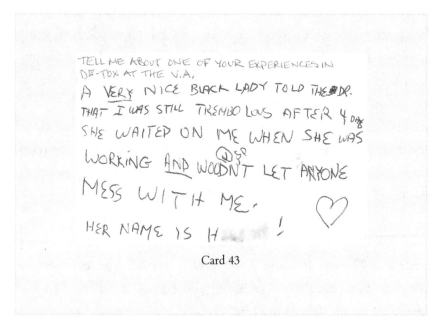

Card 43

This card is a conundrum. When I asked Lonnie about his experiences at the VA hospital, especially his detox experiences, I expected to get an earful of venom. He hated going there. He felt like a number. He couldn't get attention when he needed it—he would buzz for a nurse and one would finally show up an hour later. He hated the food. He hated having to go out on the smoking patio to have a cigarette. These were the reports Mom and I got used to hearing whenever we went to visit him. On the whole, we didn't see the neglect and indifference he railed about. We concluded that it wasn't the hospital he hated, so much as the rules and regimentation.

With all that as a backdrop, I was not expecting Lonnie to report on a nurse with such affection and appreciation. Nurse H broke the mold, showing Lonnie care beyond what he expected (although I imagine his expectations were fairly low). She let the doctor know that Lonnie was still having tremors (a common symptom in alcohol withdrawal) after four days. A more average pattern would be for the tremors to stop after two or three days. The doctor probably needed some persuading, possibly having dismissed Lonnie's complaints because they didn't seem reasonable after so many days.

In any case, Nurse H stood up for Lonnie. By his definition, that made her a hero. She waited on him—she was responsive and attentive, in other words—and wouldn't let anyone mess with him. She gave Lonnie the kind of personal care nurses are known for. Maybe she was charmed by Lonnie's smile and blue eyes; it's clear he was taken with her—"a very [underlined] nice black lady." She treated him like a person, not like a homeless drunk. It must have been sweet for him.

WHO TAUGHT YOU THE ROPES WHEN YOU WERE A KID ON
THE STREET? HOW OLD WERE YOU WHEN YOU STARTED?
BE SPECIFIC (I DON'T MEAN WHAT MOM+DAD TAUGHT US.)
YOU ASKED FOR IT!
COACH ~~~~~~~~, GREG
(WHO'S DAD WAS A WINO) & BEVERLY JO
(HEAD CHEER LEADER)
. (CHEERHEADER)
I WAS ABOUT 14 BUT I BET
YOU DON'T KNOW WHO I LOVED MOST

Card 44

Lonnie was not a "kid on the street" at age 14. In fact, he lived in a nice house on a peaceful suburban street in Topeka. We had just moved there, and in his usual fashion, Lonnie had made friends quickly. He mentions a teammate on the football team, and Beverly Jo, a cheerleader. (On an earlier card, Jo was a girl he met in the Menninger Hospital, and it was another girl he was in love with at age 14. This is the fluid nature of Lonnie's memory and sense of reality.) I have no idea what Lonnie thought the coach taught him that was useful on the street, and I'm pretty sure Greg's father was not a wino. It's very possible, though, that his was one of the liquor cabinets to which Lonnie and Greg helped themselves. From it, they could also serve whoever happened to be partying with them when the parents weren't home.

This football teammate was a player in one of Lonnie's favorite stories about himself: "How I Developed an Aversion to Mustard and Bologna." The boys had taken a bottle of vodka from Greg's house and had stopped at a convenience store to buy something to eat.

Armed with the liquor, a loaf of bread, a jar of mustard, and a package of bologna, they headed for, of course, Burnett's Mound. They spent the first half of the evening chatting, smoking, drinking vodka, and eating bologna sandwiches, and the second half throwing it all up. Lonnie never said whether or not the resulting aversion to mustard and bologna extended to vodka.

"I bet you don't know who I loved most." Me, he meant. He closed many of his cards in this way. I think he liked to anchor himself by affirming our connectedness. He wanted me to know that he loved me all the time, throughout his life, more than anyone. I knew it then, and I know it now. I miss that high-powered love, which translated into his belief that I could do anything. He made me into "The Reverend Doctor" when I was just a pastor. He made me the head of an ad agency when I was just a copywriter. To him, I was precious, beautiful; his prize possession. He believed in the idea for the book, even though it sounded crazy to him. He believed in me.

DO PEOPLE STILL CALL YOU "FATBOY" NOW THAT YOU AREN'T? WHO GAVE YOU THAT NICKNAME?

YES THEY DO! I GAVE MYSELF THAT NAME WHEN I WEIGHTED 238

I still like it. OK?

(BUT I LOVE SIS) FATBOY JOHNSON

Card 45

Mom hated people calling Lonnie "Fatboy." She thought it was mean spirited. It may well have been the result of someone making a snide remark, or, just as likely, somebody making a musical request from the audience at a bar: "Hey, fat boy, play 'Stairway to Heaven!'" Lonnie liked the name and seems to have appropriated it pretty happily. He did have a large beer gut for several years, until his health began to deteriorate, and the gut slowly faded away. I think he liked having been given a nickname—it meant he belonged, and it meant someone knew him and liked him well enough to call him by a nickname. My nickname, "Little Pink," was given to me by Lonnie in a less-than-friendly spirit, intended to suggest that I was Mom and Dad's "little pink angel" who, in stark contrast to Lonnie, never, ever got in trouble. He said it with a sneer at first, but years later we both adopted it with enthusiasm and affection.

Our dad was big on nicknames, maybe because his family had given him a nickname that stuck throughout his life: "Toots" (rhymes with "boots"). He told stories about friends from his youth called "Spaghetti" and "Jew-baby," and Army buddies called "Spook" and "Jell-O." Presumably, all these nicknames had at least a spark of reason behind them. Jew-baby was named "Julie," so her nickname was an adaptation of her actual name. Jell-O was a large fellow; Spaghetti was a skinny girl.

Nicknames were Dad's creative medium. He called Lonnie "Lumpjaw," after a huge bear in the Disney animated film "Fun and Fancy Free," which was released the year Lonnie was born. Dad called Mom "Gert," which she hated, and none of us ever knew where he got it. My nickname was Soozigut—likewise, no idea where that came from (although Susan is my middle name, so half of the nickname had identifiable roots). He called me "Sooz" and, inexplicably, "Gutweiler."

For Lonnie, nicknames were a part of life on the street. In earlier cards, he mentioned Harley Johnny and Zot. There were also Papa Smurf, Granny, Montana, and Rambo. Practically all his friends, at least the ones I ever heard about or got to meet, had alternative names. I once asked Papa Smurf what his real name was. He told me almost bashfully—Arthur—and when I said that was a good, strong name, he smiled and said it again, "Arthur." The other three or four friends of Lonnie's who were standing around with us chimed in with all their names, too. I think it felt good to them to be known, if only for a few moments, as the person they were pre-street, pre-alcohol, pre-drugs, pre-disaster.

"But I love Sis." He's reattaching again, as he has on several other cards, and using an affectionate nickname for me. He liked his nickname, but he *loved* his sis.

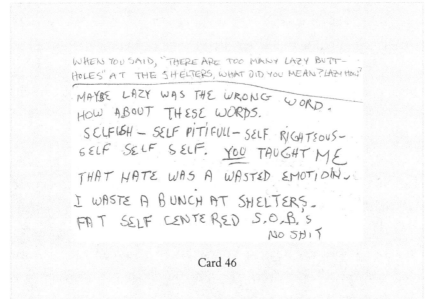

WHEN YOU SAID, "THERE ARE TOO MANY LAZY BUTT-
HOLES" AT THE SHELTERS, WHAT DID YOU MEAN? LAZY HOW?

MAYBE LAZY WAS THE WRONG WORD.
HOW ABOUT THESE WORDS.
SELFISH — SELF PITIFULL— SELF RIGHTEOUS—
SELF SELF SELF. YOU TAUGHT ME
THAT HATE WAS A WASTED EMOTION.
I WASTE A BUNCH AT SHELTERS.
FAT SELF CENTERED S.O.B.'s
                    NO SHIT

Card 46

The earlier card, on which Lonnie had referred to the "lazy buttholes" at the shelters, was so jarring that I had to follow up. I had heard him fume about this before, so I knew it wasn't just a random bit of hostility. I was offended until I stopped to consider that homeless people could be "buttholes" just as well as anyone else, but I needed to know what Lonnie meant.

His language on this card is uncharacteristically coarse. In fact, this is one of only three or four cards on which he uses any sort of expletives. His handwriting and spelling, along with his articulate, controlled expression of his thoughts, suggests that he was reasonably sober (only partially drunk) when he wrote this. But it's obvious that he was thoroughly revved up by the end of his answer.

I suspect that he had had a recent run-in at a shelter. He rarely went to the shelters to sleep—only if it was bitterly cold or raining torrentially, and even then, he surely would have exhausted every alternative, including every friend and acquaintance who might offer a porch or backyard. Self-pity would have repulsed Lonnie. I heard him talk about himself with self-deprecation, sometimes (especially in the later cards) sadness or wistfulness, but never with self-pity. Most often, Lonnie was cocky about his ability to take care of himself, as though his sheer survival proved daily that he was capable and independent.

Self-righteous, preachy, condescending people were, I'm sure, plentiful on the street, where respect was scarce and self-respect the scarcest of all. "I'm better than you" would be a tasty statement relished by someone who had little reason and less opportunity to say the words. It is easy to imagine Lonnie, when his circumstances drove him to stay in a shelter overnight, thinking of another person in the same situation, "I'm better than you."

Lonnie was amazingly unselfish in some ways. He was happy to share what he had with friends. For example, he usually got some silly little toys or other trinkets in his Christmas stocking. (Yes, we hung them up with care every year, and Mom and I continued this tradition right through her last Christmas.) One thing he got every year was a toy car, always red. This started when he was a little boy. He frequently announced that one day he would be rich and have a little red sports car. So, he received one every year for Christmas. He told us one year that he had taken his loot back down to his neighborhood and "played Santa," handing out new pairs of socks to friends and giving away the little red car and other trinkets and candy to "some street kids." I don't doubt this.

Lonnie never failed to bring each of us a gift when he came to Mom and Dad's house for Christmas. One year, my gift was a small, sterling silver cross on a sterling silver chain; he removed it from around his neck and handed it to me. I don't know where he got it, but he told me he had been wearing it for weeks, tucked safely under his gnarly beard, to keep it from getting stolen. (I know he was not exaggerating: It took me an hour to get all the hair out of the chain.) Sometimes his gifts were handmade cards, other years he had bought some little trinket. But he never came empty-handed.

BESIDES AT CHRISTMAS, WHERE DO YOU GET CLOTHES?

PEOPLE ON THE STREETS EXCHANGE CLOTHES. WE ALL KNOW EACH OTHERS SIZE'S!

HOW ABOUT THAT!?

LJ

Card 47

Here is Lonnie's imagination at its sunniest. I know Lonnie impulsively gave away his socks and other possessions whenever he had the chance. He owned so little, I suppose, that ownership had little significance for him. I suspect the feeling of being able to give something away gave him the same satisfaction that generosity gives anyone. When he says street people exchange clothes and know each other's sizes, he is envisioning a free-flowing hippie-esque community in which everyone is as loosely tied to their possessions as he is.

But on other cards he talks about being rolled for his bug spray, backpack, or even his cane. Later, his VA-provided wheelchair made him an easy target and a tempting one. A wheelchair, unlike whatever else a street person might possess, could actually be pawned, in spite of the stamp on the back, "Property of the Veterans Administration."

Lonnie and the others may well have exchanged clothes through the clothing banks maintained by local charities and churches in Houston and every other large city. Clothes are distributed according to need and the weather—most places with harsh winter weather hold coat or blanket drives. Frigid nights are rare in Houston, but when they do occur, vans circulate, handing out whatever they can to whomever they can find in an effort to help them stay warm.

Size was barely relevant, as long as the clothing was not too small. In fact, large clothing accommodated the layering that kept all of Lonnie's clothes in his immediate possession all the time. Lonnie often wore everything he owned, no matter how hot the weather. (With the advent of fees for carryon luggage, airline travelers have only recently caught on to the concept of wearing their entire wardrobe!)

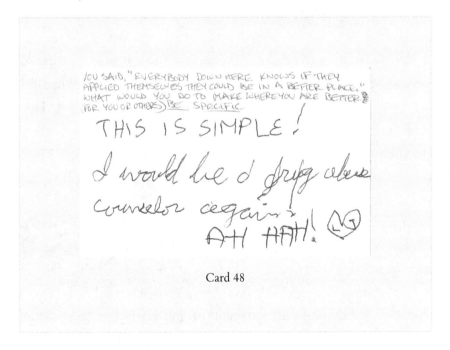

Card 48

This question came from a phone conversation I had with Lonnie—one of the few, since I couldn't call him and he was not always able to stay sober, gather two quarters, and find a pay phone all at once. We tried various approaches to being able to talk more regularly, including me getting a private toll-free number that only Lonnie had, and, later, me sending him pre-paid phone cards so he could call without a quarter. We quickly learned that phone cards were easy to steal and in high demand. The toll-free number had to stay in Lonnie's memory in order for him to use it—not a reliable system, as it turned out. I suggested he get a tattoo (he already had several, so I figured one 10-digit number would hardly be noticeable). But even if he could have remembered the number, he still would have had to arrange to be near a pay phone. This became more difficult over time, not only because of Lonnie's diminishing mobility but also because, in hopes of making it harder for drug dealers to do business anonymously, city officials eliminated pay phones.

The planets aligned occasionally, and everything came together so we could have a long conversation. I cherished those talks. The rule, as it was at Mom's house, was that he be sober when he called. That made it possible to talk like brothers and sisters do—like *only* brothers and sisters can. We talked about the old times. We talked about Mom and her health, about our relatives, Uncle Strange, Auntie Ric-Tic, and the snot twins. (We were the family of nicknames, remember.) We talked about each other's lives, and in those talks, Lonnie was as inquisitive about my life as I was about his. Lonnie once asked me the same question I asked him: Don't you ever get tired of the hassles and want to change your life? We both admitted that we did.

I tossed back to him his statement on this card—that he could be in a better place if he applied himself. His better place was to "be a drug counselor again." He is thinking of the cautionary role he took on with the kids at the Covenant House, an unofficial yet influential role. He told me he liked being the laboratory case of how not to end up, and he got a kick out of seeing the impact he had on the kids by the thunderstruck looks on their faces.

He had a gift for connecting with people no matter the circumstances. Friends at the church our family attended in Houston remember Lonnie fondly from the times he came to Christmas Eve communion services with us over the years. It's a nice little church in a nice middle-class suburb, filled with people who are not accustomed to homeless men sitting next to them in the pews. It is a tribute to the charity of those friends, and maybe the effect of seeing Lonnie on Christmas Eve of all nights, that Lonnie was welcomed cordially and made to feel accepted and cared about. Until years later when his mobility was severely impaired and his alcoholism had taken a massive toll on his ability to function, Lonnie rarely missed a Christmas Eve service with us, and when he did, people invariably asked about him.

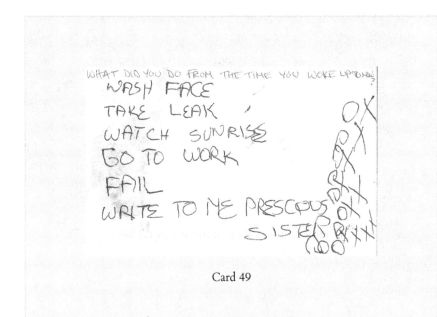

Card 49

Lonnie's darkest card is hard to look at, even from a distance of many years. I am sorry he had that day. He didn't deserve it.

I sent Lonnie this same question several times, and the answers weren't the only things that differed drastically. On Card 1, his handwriting is small and precise, controlled, and the lines are fairly straight. He lays out the day in detail, including the precise time and duration of each entry. His day holds both accomplishment (three "jobs") and relaxation, and it ends with a cheer as he organizes his bag and writes to his "fine sister."

Card 49 reads more like a to-do list than a series of journal entries. Lonnie has scrawled it in short, crude outbursts: "WASH FACE," "TAKE LEAK." There is a peaceful moment while he watches the sunrise. He goes to work. He fails. He writes to his precious sister. Without the fifth line, the card would be brusque but vaguely familiar. Wash face and take leak: Ordinary morning routine, like anybody else. Watch sunrise: contemplative, inspiring way to start the day. Go to work: As average as it gets.

And then, "FAIL." He reports it as matter-of-factly as he does "take a leak," as though it were an ordinary part of any day, and he moves without drama to the conclusion of his day, writing the postcard to his precious sister. He closes with 10 hugs and 10 kisses, more than on any other card so far.

This may be the best sketch of Lonnie's life contained on any of the cards. It registers his acceptance of life as it came at him moment by moment—the physical necessities, the beauty, the practicality, the darkness, and the love. He ends the card by sending me a gift of Xs and Os. It is a full and authentic portrait.

4

July 1994

I was irritated when I received this card. I had asked this question
before, because I was curious about the whole process. It was
effectively another way of asking "How did this happen?" I felt only
Lonnie could have answered the question, so I didn't appreciate
someone else answering for him.

WHEN DID YOU FIRST START LIVING ON THE STREET
IN MONTROSE? WHO SHOWED YOU THE ROPES?

MARY L. ___ (GRANNY)
1948 – 19 – – –
I TAUGHT LONNIE EVEVERY-
THING HE KNOWS. (TO THIS
DAY & DATE)

♡ LONNIE

Card 50

Lonnie really couldn't answer the question. He wasn't able to say when he had started living on the street—on an earlier card, he said it was something that mostly evolved. I don't know how that could happen. Did he not notice that he didn't have a place to sleep or go to the bathroom or eat a snack? Becoming homeless is a thing that I'd notice and, having noticed, I'd want to reverse it. Not Lonnie, though.

On another card, he described it as "a Robin Hood thing." The rich were not being robbed nor the poor distributed to, but the romance of a beneficent outlaw life was a perfect fit for Olaf, the Viking hero. Lonnie saw his lifestyle as according him maximum freedom. To me his life appeared anything but free; still, it did allow him to live without bills, a boss, hours, schedules, or responsibilities of any kind. Free to roam Sherwood Forest (or the North Sea, or Montrose), he could do as he pleased. Naturally, then, as he drifted (evolved) into the homeless "lifestyle," he would see little about it to make him want to turn around.

Lonnie had known "Granny" for many years, and she may have been a mentor, teaching Lonnie her survival tricks and secrets. It's clear the two were friends, or Lonnie would not have let her get her hands on one of his cards. In a letter written at the same time he sent these postcards, he said he was sending a few cards from friends who wanted to "help" him. (The quotation marks are his.) Lonnie reclaimed this card, however—maybe reassuring me (and himself) that he was in control of the situation—with his signature, "(Heart), Lonnie."

The idea of having a mentor to teach you how to be homeless seems incongruous. If you had few possessions and limited resources, you would expect to compete for resources, not have someone helpfully pointing you toward them. But how else did Lonnie discover that urine could calm red ant bites, or that one merchant (and not another) would allow him to sleep behind his dumpster, or that a particular server at a particular restaurant had a soft heart and would sneak food to a homeless man with deep blue eyes? Trial and error can't account for all of it. But why would someone tell him about that soft-hearted server, knowing that if too many people asked it might shut down the source for everyone?

It makes a little more sense when I think of how highly Lonnie prized the status attached to his "counselor" relationship with the kids at Covenant House. Unofficial though it was, Lonnie's testimony may have been some of the most influential counsel those kids received, and it is certain that Lonnie savored being able to confer something like wisdom upon them. Likewise, Granny, who had been on the street for a long time, might find it satisfying to be able to conduct orientation for a new guy. Being a mentor no doubt felt valuable and dignified.

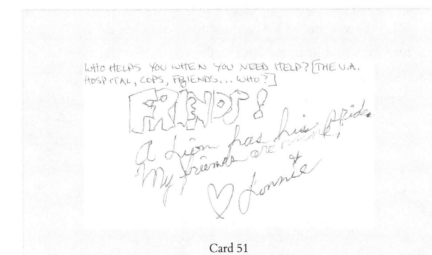

Card 51

Asking Lonnie who helped him when he needed help allowed him to give just the kind of answer he gave: sunny, even a little boastful. "A lion has his pride," he purrs, "my friends are mine." Lonnie drew people in easily, and he had a cadre of friends who hung out with him a lot of the time. However, when Lonnie was mugged, knifed or having a seizure, it was often the nearest police officer who called the ambulance for him. Friends helped with certain things—cigarettes or a light, a little change for a beer or a phone call. Some of his friends were from another time in his life, when he associated regularly with people who had addresses. A few of them still lived in the Montrose area, and if asked, would allow Lonnie a couch or at least a porch, and might give him a meal, a shower, maybe even a couple of dollars.

He had other friends, however, who could only be referred to as friends with quotes around the word. These "friends" were sharp enough to see that Lonnie was trusting, even gullible. One such person was Dina (I changed her name to avoid a lawsuit, though I'd gladly have the world know her character), a woman Lonnie met when he was in the VA hospital for a round of detox. She was charmed by him, I imagine, but she also knew an opportunity when she saw one.

Lonnie had finally found his way to the VA department that could help him apply for disability payments from the government. He had never been able to do this before, mostly because he had zero tolerance for any kind of administrative process. Typically, the first time he was shunted from one bureaucrat to another, he threw up his hands and walked away. Mom and I kept urging him, and I made a few phone calls to find out exactly the right person for him to talk to. Eventually, he figured he'd find that person and try out the system again. This time he was successful but hit a snag—he needed a way to cash the checks, and he had no checking account.

I wrote out instructions for him on how to open a checking account. I explained them carefully and assured him that he would be perfectly capable of doing it on his own. He seemed confident he could take care of it. He said he knew a bank near the hospital; he would have his checks sent to the hospital and held for him, then pick them up and take them straight to the bank to deposit them. Mom and I were hopeful.

When we talked to him next, he reported that he had found another, easier way to handle it. Dina, it turned out, had been his confidant throughout the process of applying for the payments, lending a sympathetic ear when he mentioned the difficulty of cashing the checks. She would cash them for him, she said, if he would just sign them over to her. She and a girlfriend would let Lonnie move into their apartment, he would pay a share of the rent, and Dina would manage Lonnie's money, giving him cash, of course, whenever he wanted it.

In retrospect, Mom and I shouldn't have been surprised when Lonnie started complaining about not being able to get his money from Dina. She would pick up the check, cash it and Lonnie would never see another trace of it. I called Dina once to find out if there was some sort of misunderstanding. There wasn't—she was stealing his money. She bought herself a new car, using Lonnie's money for the payments. He finally got fed up and moved out, but he had no idea how to undo her check scam.

I got on the phone to the VA and told them exactly what was happening. Could I be his co-signer, I wanted to know, since I was a blood relative? Yes, but I had to go, *in person*, to the VA offices to make the change, and I had to have a form signed by him saying that he authorized me to be the co-signer. It was daunting, but doable, and once we got the paperwork done and the arrangements were made, Lonnie was astonished to discover how much money he had—a little more than $800 a month. I don't know whether the VA was ever able to catch up with Dina. I wonder how many other veterans she had stolen from using the same con.

How was Lonnie, so savvy in the ways of the street, taken in by such an obvious con? She knew how to make Lonnie feel needed, perhaps, and she played on his readiness to be attached to someone. She was a lot younger than him—maybe he saw her as a kid and couldn't quite conceive of a kid being cold or calculating.

Once Lonnie's checks were assigned over to me, I could cash them for him and give him the cash all at once or as he needed it. But he never wanted a lot of money at once. Of course, once it became known that he might be carrying money on the street, he would become a prime target. So, the most he ever wanted was $20. I put his checks into my checking account and, when he called Mom to ask her to have me send him some of his money, I'd mail cash to him at the flower shop address. This system worked pretty well but didn't last long. Something in the VA paperwork had to be renewed annually, and since I lived too far away to coordinate the process, my co-signer status expired. I don't know what became of his checks after that.

Lonnie wasn't bothered by the lapse in the banking system we had created. He simply didn't have that much interest in having money. What would he need it for, really? Having money didn't automatically prompt him to say, "Maybe now I can find an apartment or room to rent and I'd have a place to stay." He was not inclined, as I would be, to want his own place to sleep. That would have required regular rent payments. There was little he would buy, since most of what he needed he could get for free—food in the dumpster, cigarettes in outdoor ashtrays where people discarded perfectly good, half-smoked butts. Maybe he could buy a six-pack to share with his "pride."

Lonnie and his friends helped each other feel normal. They sat together at the bus stop or on a curb, smoking or passing around a bottle of beer or wine. They listened to Lonnie, commiserated with him, laughed with him—they couldn't help liking him. But the way people could appear and disappear randomly on the street, it just didn't pay to be friends without the quotation marks.

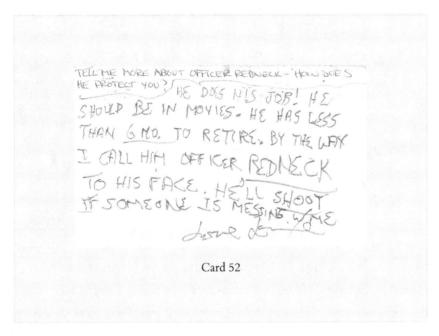

Card 52

After Lonnie died in 2005, I visited the storefront police station on Montrose near Lonnie's corner. "Officer Redneck" had long since retired, but I met several officers who remembered Lonnie, "the old guy in the wheelchair." One said he was a good guy at heart. Another chimed in amicably that Lonnie had given them a good bit of trouble over the years.

I asked them to show me a printout of his rap sheet, the list of all his arrests and the outcome of the charges. Most of the offenses had to do with public intoxication, mouthing off to an officer or having to use an alley or shrub as a toilet—the kind of things that landed Lonnie in city or county jail for his three hots and a cot. Occasionally the sentences were longer. During those stays, Lonnie often ended up in the VA hospital at one time or another for detox and some combination of therapy, training, and physical rehabilitation for his leg, or simply to be treated for one of the many chronic ailments he suffered from. He had cellulitis, almost impossible to avoid when you can't keep your skin dry, much less clean. He had bronchitis, a combination of his lifestyle, the weather, and decades of cigarette smoking. On any given day, he also might have broken bones, lacerations, bruises, and other injuries that resulted from a mugging or some battle he felt he had to fight. Still, he didn't like being in the hospital any more than being in jail—it was all incarceration.

Officer Redneck may have been one of the police officers who treated Lonnie with some courtesy and, perhaps, a bit of humor. They must have had some conversation, since Lonnie knew the officer was approaching retirement. Maybe he looked the other way when Lonnie needed to relieve himself and the only facility available was somebody's hedge. Maybe he chased away some punk who menaced Lonnie or eyed his cane or wheelchair. Lonnie has raised this officer to hero status, gleefully envisioning the officer shooting anybody who messed with him. Authority-phobe that he was, Lonnie must have found it fascinating that he could have something like a friendship with a police officer.

Card 53

The thief stole the cane while Lonnie was sleeping, but from the sound of it, he wasn't quite stealthy enough. Lonnie said he got the cane back because the thief was scared. Maybe Officer Redneck made an appearance. Maybe Lonnie growled and flashed a bicep pumped up and hardened by bracing his weight on the cane when he walked.

The contemptible nature of the theft is typical of the kind of opportunistic, in-the-moment crime that was commonplace in Lonnie's world. The cane was of little value to the thief. It couldn't be pawned, Lonnie said, and a cane can be purchased at a drug store for a few dollars, or at a dollar store for even less. Walking around with a cane, Lonnie was conspicuously vulnerable. He had only one good leg and he moved slowly. A good shove would send him tumbling, at which time even a child could grab whatever Lonnie dropped and run off before he could find his feet again.

Lonnie closes the card with 13 kisses and 13 hugs, more than all the other cards, and a fat heart. "There, there," he says to his little sister, "don't feel sad or discouraged." All those kisses and hugs dispel the bitterness of such a mean crime, replacing it with Lonnie's reassurance of love and connection—always connection. Many of his cards seem to say, "Don't worry, I'm the big brother and I'll be fine." It worked. I was always willing to be the starry-eyed little sister to his strong, protective . . . heroic . . . big brother.

Card 54

No, he never considered changing his lifestyle. Not just "No," but "NO!"

Had he said yes, it would have been tantalizing. I would have tried to figure out how I could help him to make whatever change he was thinking about. I would have wondered what a different Lonnie would be like. I would have reimagined him. In fact, when I wrote the card, I was hoping for a different answer. I had already begun to reimagine him.

The postscript is an enigma. Our dad would have been thrilled if Lonnie had decided to change his lifestyle at any point. He loved

Lonnie, but he struggled to maintain an open mind as the gulf between himself and Lonnie widened, and their lifestyles diverged to the point of being irreconcilable. Lonnie had no responsibilities; Dad was the family breadwinner. Lonnie answered to no one; Dad had a wife, kids, a boss, neighbors, friends, church—all depending on him in various ways. Dad coped with things by being the Stoic, clenching his teeth a little tighter and being a little tougher; Lonnie coped by drinking, withdrawing, or fighting. Lonnie could claim no profession or career; he considered himself a musician, but his music wasn't making him a living. Dad built a career from a first job as a steel mill worker to a regional industrial engineer, learning what he needed to know along the way, on the job. When he lost his job in 1968, it undid him. Lonnie never held any job longer than a couple of years—that's how long he worked as a newspaper vendor on the median strip somewhere in Montrose.

They had a lot in common, though, and much of it was useful to Lonnie on the street. They were resilient and resourceful, always proving themselves. Both were easygoing, intelligent, and charismatic, especially with women. Both enjoyed being around other people.

The biggest point of divergence was their understanding of what it meant to be independent. Lonnie believed he was independent because he was accountable to no one. Dad believed Lonnie was totally dependent—on charity, on his parents, on people giving him handouts. For Dad, independence meant earning a living, supporting himself and his family. But for Lonnie, that seemed like the ultimate dependency—needing that paycheck to survive meant being enslaved to the boss, the company, and the schedule.

When Lonnie was a young boy, he and Dad shared an interest in sports, especially football. Lonnie was a Boy Scout. He was crazy about cars, first model cars and then the real things. When Lonnie went into the Army, Dad thought it would help him mature, learn discipline, and become self-confident. Those are the things Dad believed the Army had done for himself, although this idea conflicted with certain facts. For example, Dad had gotten out of the Army early by charming a young woman clerk into adding his name to a discharge list. The list went all the way through the alphabet, and there, at the bottom after the Zs, was "Johnson, Lloyd."

Lonnie had made Dad proud many times as a kid, especially on the football field. Lonnie's grades were pretty good, at least until he hit high school (except in areas like "Attendance" and "Behavior"). He was a successful Boy Scout, although he stopped short of becoming an Eagle Scout. He was even a good churchgoer, even after he was allowed to decide for himself whether or not he would go to church with the family.

When Lonnie went into the Army, he progressed through basic training and received his Private First Class rank. Then he trained for the Army Corps of Engineers, following in Dad's engineer footsteps. He graduated from the training, and, at the graduation ceremony at Fort Leonard Wood, Missouri, seemed appropriately full of himself. Dad's plan seemed to be taking hold.

Soon after his graduation, Lonnie shipped overseas, to Germany. The year was 1965, in the thick of the Vietnam War. I was mostly unaware of the war; if Mom and Dad worried about Lonnie being sent into combat duty, they never revealed that to me. However, for Lonnie, the dangers of being so far away from home were much more immediate.

Dad's plan had not taken into account that Lonnie was an immature, 17-year-old boy when he entered the Army. He made friends fast, winning their admiration, as he always had, by breaking rules. Eventually, encouraged by his bravado, they probably undertook a game of can-you-top-this. By the time Lonnie turned 18, he was a smoker, a hard drinker, and a low-grade criminal with a long list of minor military offenses. His discharge was general, which for Dad was both a disappointment (he would have preferred honorable status) and a relief compared to the dishonorable discharge Lonnie probably deserved. His discharging officer was lenient, recognizing that Lonnie's main offense was being an immature kid.

It's not clear whether Lonnie ever grew out of that misbehaving teenager frame of mind. By the end of his life, he was wearying of the stresses of living from moment to moment. But he didn't get weary enough to prompt him to try to change. NO!

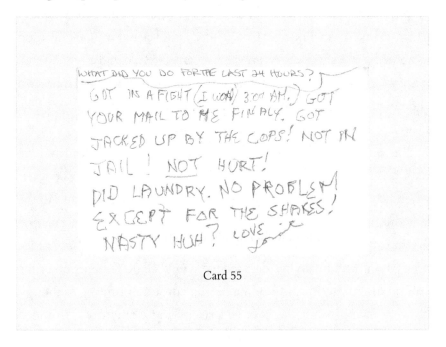

Card 55

Fighting was simply a part of life for Lonnie, made inevitable by his drinking and the need to prove that he was not as easy a mark as he appeared. He was 47, but with his graying hair and weathered skin, he looked much older. His cane, by this time a constant, was as much a weapon as a walking aid. When he got into a fight at 3 a.m., it's likely he was drunk and took on someone who offended him or tried to "mess with him"—stealing his stuff, knocking over his beer can. It didn't take much to provoke Lonnie when he was drunk.

He specifies that he won, and that he was not hurt, but goes on to say that he was "jacked up" by the cops. In other words, the cops intervened. Although they were not particularly sympathetic to Lonnie, they decided not to put him in jail. Maybe it was just more trouble than it was worth; surely at some point they got tired of dealing with him.

He did his laundry—by that time it must have been daylight and getting to be time for a drink. Tremors reminded him that he hadn't had a drink in an hour or two, and alcohol acted as a medication to remedy the shakes and prevent seizures. He could dose himself with a can or two of beer, even light beer, and would seem normal and coherent. If he went more than a few hours without alcohol, he seized.

The semi-medical use of alcohol became apparent to Mom and me on Christmas Eve of the last year Mom required Lonnie to be sober when he came to her house. I had picked him up on his corner in the late afternoon; we had had a light dinner and spent a quiet evening visiting and reminiscing. Lonnie's shakes progressed noticeably as the time passed, and finally we decided we would all go to bed. Sometime around midnight, I heard Lonnie in his bedroom, grunting as though he were trying to lift the bed. In a sleepy fog of my own, I tiptoed down the hall to his room, knocked, and called his name. Now I could hear him clearly, groaning more than grunting, and when I entered the room, I saw that his body was rigid and shaking, his face was deep red, and he was bleeding from his mouth. Abruptly snapping awake, I figured out that he must have bitten his tongue or lip, and that he was having a seizure. I called an ambulance and woke Mom, telling her what was happening to Lonnie, and assuring her that the ambulance was coming. The ambulance (and a fire truck and a police car) arrived in just a few minutes, and off we went to follow the ambulance to the VA hospital. Lonnie was given Dilantin and quickly hooked up to an IV and other monitors and devices. We stayed with him until the doctors told us he was stable, out of danger, and ready to be admitted. Then we took a quiet ride home, our thoughts too unsettled to be spoken out loud. We returned to the hospital Christmas afternoon to take Lonnie his presents.

The next year, Mom stocked the Christmas day refrigerator with light beer, and the three of us had a peaceful and merry Christmas.

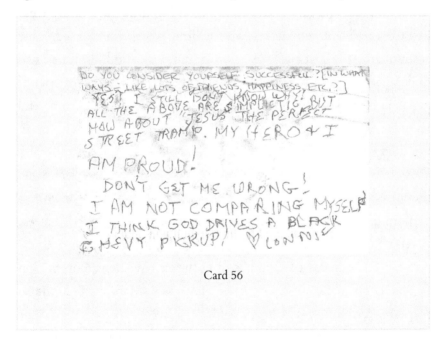

Card 56

By mid-1994, I had begun to talk about feeling that I was called to ministry. My cancer surgery and treatments were past, and the outcome had been good, so I was about ready to apply for admission to seminary. I had begun working on the official process for ordination and getting more eager and excited by the day. Lonnie knew this; maybe that's why Jesus came to his mind so incongruously. He doesn't sound sober on this card; his mind was free to meander.

Asking Lonnie whether he considered himself a success was like asking if he considered himself fashionable. It wasn't something he gave a lot of thought to, and he certainly didn't strive toward it. I offered a few examples—lots of friends, happiness—because I wasn't sure he would have a concept of what success was for him. The question and the examples I provided were nearly meaningless to him, "simplictic," as he pointed out. For Lonnie, success would include friends and happiness, but considering how those terms were defined on the street, success was a little more complicated. One component of success was simple survival, and Lonnie was undeniably successful by that measure. He had the kind of friends and happiness that were possible on the street—friends who came and went according to what he had to offer them, happiness that hung on not being hungry, hot, wet, or in withdrawal.

He offers up a little theology: "What about Jesus, the perfect street tramp? My hero, and I am proud!" What about Jesus? I take him to be pointing out that Jesus had nothing—none of the signs of success common to Jesus' time or to ours, such as status, wealth, or political power. "Foxes have holes, and birds of the air have nests; but the Son of Man has nowhere to lay his head," Jesus said (Matthew 8:20). Jesus was homeless; this was Lonnie's truth.

He made a point of stating that he was not comparing himself to Jesus, at least not in the sense of being perfect, sinless, or holy. Lonnie knew Jesus, though, in a very direct way.

The black Chevy pickup truck is a powerful symbol for Lonnie. He told me about a dream he'd had involving a supernatural black pickup truck. In the dream, he was standing around with some friends on the sidewalk when this black pickup truck pulled up. In the back were our grandparents, Dad, several of Lonnie's street friends, kids from his troubled high school days, all riding around in the truck, partying. When the truck pulled up near Lonnie, everyone in the back started calling to him, waving him toward the truck. He saw that the driver was Jesus, who was smiling and calling Lonnie's name. He said it looked like fun, but he had to pass for now.

I asked him what he thought the dream meant, and he said it was pretty obvious: he wasn't ready to die just yet. But when he was ready, he figured Jesus himself and all the people he loved would be there to give him a ride to heaven in the party truck.

DO YOU GET LONELY, EVEN THOUGH YOU HAVE A LOT OF PEOPLE AROUND? "OH YES! IF I HAVE $ I HAVE TOO MANY "FRIENDS" + IF I DON'T I HAVE GOOD FRIENDS WHO ALWAYS WANT TO LECTURE ME. YOU KNOW HOW I HATE THAT! SO I AM LONELY MOST OF THE TIME, MY MOST HAPPY TIMES ARE W/ MY 50 OR SO PIDGEONS WHO EAT OUT OF MY HAND + LIGHT ON ME WITHOUT LEAVING DROPPINGS. THEY HAVE PEACEFUL + REASSURING VOICES. FAR OUT! YES I GET VERY LONELY

Card 57

A couple of weeks after he was thinking about the heavenly pickup truck, Lonnie was back in reality, and sober. Both the content and the handwriting on this card confirm it. Yes, he got lonely, surrounded by so-called friends who wanted to enjoy whatever money (or beer, or cigarettes) he had, or if he didn't have money, friends who wanted to lecture him. He was right, I *do* know how he hated that.

He could barely tolerate it from our parents—Dad in particular, who was prone to lecturing in spite of being an affectionate and loving parent. My behavior was rarely the topic ("Little Pink Angel," remember), but I heard plenty of the lectures aimed at my big brother. When he got going really well, Dad got into what Lonnie and I came to recognize as the "Three Pillars" speech. Dad had three pillars of his life, he said: God, family, and country, in that order. It was deeply true of Dad. He was very duty-oriented, and he expected Lonnie and me to embrace the same orientation and the same pillars. Lonnie idolized Dad; it showed in many of his postcards. But in the moment, what I remember Lonnie doing in response to one of Dad's speeches on responsibility was rolling his eyes.

"I am lonely most of the time." No wonder Lonnie takes such pleasure in the companionship of "his" pigeons. They eat out of his hand (they are the hungry ones; he is the benefactor). They light on him "without leaving droppings" (they seek him out, they offer affection, they trust him, and he can trust them). He talks about them respectfully and with deep appreciation for the way they treat him. He doesn't use crude language where he could, and instead indicates that they are gentle and considerate, using polite language that matches their "peaceful and reassuring" voices. I saw him with his pigeons once. They seemed comfortable in each other's company.

WHERE DO YOU KEEP YOUR STUFF?

MOSTLY ON ME, IT IS
TERRIFICALLY HARD TO KEEP MY THINGS
FROM BEING STOLEN BECAUSE THERE ARE SO
MANY PEOPLE ON THE STREET W/ ABSO-
LUTELY NO MORALS. ONE NIGHT I SPRAYED
MYSELF W/ "OFF" + LAID MY HEAD DOWN ON MY
BACK PACK, WITHOUT MOSQUITOES I SLEPT TOO
GOOD + WOKE UP W/ MY HEAD ON A LOG, THE
NEXT DAY I SAW A CUTE LITTLE GIRL
WEARING IT. NOTHING I COULD DO, SHE
HAD SOLD MY STUFF + PUT IN HERS! DLJ

Card 58

Grocery carts, plastic lawn bags, and large backpacks are ways to ensure that you know where all your stuff is at all times. What few things Lonnie didn't want to carry around with him, he stashed in secret hiding places on roofs, in tall weeds, or underneath dumpsters. Still, those spots were only for things that were replaceable but not worth anything for reselling, like underwear, crackers, or candy bars, or personal items like a comb or nail clippers. Prized possessions like family pictures, cigarettes, cash, identification cards, and the postcards stayed at his fingertips.

"People with absolutely no morals"—they lived on the street, too. The collision between amorality and desperation made theft look like a reasonable option and made Lonnie believe the idea of spraying himself with "Off" before going to sleep was unwise. Biting mosquitoes would have kept him just wakeful enough to rouse if someone tried to pull his backpack out from under his head and replace it with a log.

The cute little girl thief was probably real enough to Lonnie, and there actually were children living on the street right alongside their parents. She may also be the little girl who draws on one of Lonnie's later cards, or the recurring pregnant 13-year-old, or some amalgam of children Lonnie had met on the street or somewhere else or in some other era of his life. Stealing the backpack, selling Lonnie's stuff, and replacing it with her own is exactly how it would go, and, as Lonnie said, there was little he could do about it. If the thief really was a little girl, Lonnie would be hard pressed to take any action, even if it were available to him. He had a soft spot in his daddy heart for little girls, especially lost ones.

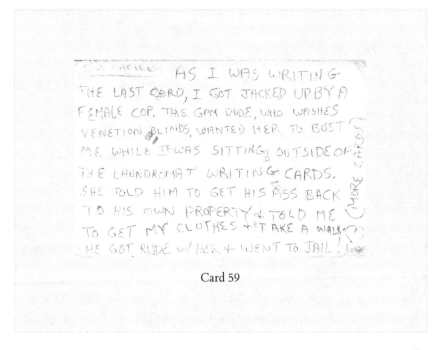

AS I WAS WRITING THE LAST CARD, I GOT JACKED UP BY A FEMALE COP. THIS GAY DUDE, WHO WASHES VENETION BLINDS, WANTED HER TO BUST ME WHILE I WAS SITTING OUTSIDE OF THE LAUNDROMAT WRITING CARDS. SHE TOLD HIM TO GET HIS ASS BACK TO HIS OWN PROPERTY & TOLD ME TO GET MY CLOTHES + TAKE A WALK. HE GOT RUDE W/ HER + WENT TO JAIL! (MORE CARDS)

Card 59

Lonnie makes a mini movie on this card. His writing ability is plainly visible in the way he includes selected details (the gay dude washed venetian blinds), the economy of his storytelling, the momentum.

People frequently called in complaints about Lonnie, mostly to get him away from their businesses so their customers wouldn't be scared off. The neighborhood cops may have lost patience with Lonnie now and then, but, based on this story, they also got tired of the locals calling them every time he sat down somewhere. This officer did the wisest thing in the situation—she dispersed both men. But, unlike Lonnie, the complainant mouthed off to the cop and ended up in jail. What a kick for Lonnie! Normally he would be the one mouthing off, and the one spending the night on a city-provided cot. His amusement is barely disguised.

Not being allowed to sit down anywhere is exhausting. I once portrayed a beggar in a church presentation of Bethlehem. The city marketplace was replicated on the church lawn, and the cast included the holy family, dozens of tradespeople (bakers, potters), farmers, shepherds, and a group of Roman soldiers whose job it was to protect the townspeople from riffraff like me. For the three hours of the event, I was not allowed to sit down, nor even to stand still in front of anyone's shop. The Roman soldiers, striving for authenticity as avidly as I, rushed to the aid of anyone who complained, jostling me away and poking me with their spears to keep me moving along. In mid-December, the bonfire at one end of the "town" offered welcome warmth, but I could only stand next to it for a moment or two before someone objected to my odious presence. It made me tired and irritable, and, finally, angry and hostile. I had to tolerate this for three hours, and by the time it had passed, I was grateful just to be left alone.

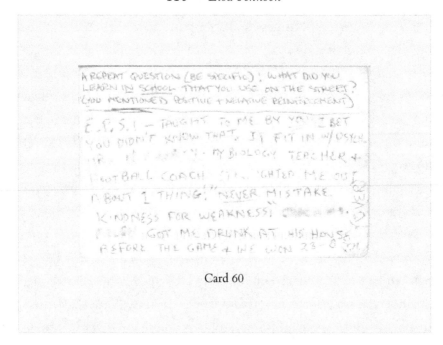

Card 60

I don't know what E.P.S.I. is. I've Googled it, asked friends, pored over letters—I taught it to him, he said, but if so, there is a blank space in my memory where it used to live.

He credits his biology teacher and coach with teaching him that kindness and weakness are not the same thing. How did he use this learning on the street? Maybe he applied it by showing kindness without fearing that it would make him look vulnerable, although that seems risky for someone who was, in fact, physically vulnerable. The other coach Lonnie mentions was a real person, but the rest of that story is almost certainly fictitious. Lonnie drank in high school, maybe even before football games. With his considerable athletic talent, he may have been able to play drunk. But his coach was not his supplier.

Card 60

The breathless story spilled onto the back of the card, where Lonnie delivered the climactic line, "I scored all four touchdowns." Then he added his real punchline: "Dad was proud." His thoughts went from E.P.S.I. and me, to kindness vs. weakness, to drinking, to scoring the winning touchdown (and all the others as well), to Dad being proud. He ended that train of thought at the point most likely to have been 100 percent true.

Lonnie was in jail six days out of any given month, sometimes, as he notes on Card 61, "on purpose." For him, the private cell was a luxury—it was clean and dry, it came with not only food and a bed, but also a toilet, a sink, and a few personal hygiene items. The cops may have realized they were providing free room and board for Lonnie (and who knows how many other homeless people). It's possible they resented the con, or the expense to taxpayers, or the additional paperwork. But when the police received a trespassing complaint from a citizen, they didn't have a choice.

ON AVERAGE, OVER A MONTH, HOW MUCH TIME DO YOU
SPEND IN JAIL? WHAT KINDS OF CHARGES — NAME
AS MANY DIFFERENT CHARGES AS YOU CAN.

SIX. AVERAGE, SOME TIMES I GO ON
PURPOSE. THE DOCTORS GIVE ME A PRI-
VATE CELL BECAUSE I HAVE SIEZURES, I USUALLY
GET OUT THE NEXT DAY — CHARGES:
SIMPLE ASSAULT - PUBLIC INTOXICATION - ABUS-
IVE LANGUAGE - CONSUMING ALC. ON UNLICENED
PREMISE. FAILURE TO APPEAR IN COURT ON
TICKETS. CRIMINAL TRESPASSING.
THATS ABOUT IT.   LONNIE

Card 61

It is surprising that Lonnie listed "simple assault" at the top of his list. It may be that this was the most recent charge he had incurred, so it was top of mind. But a swipe of his cane at somebody who bothered him would constitute simple assault, and that must have been a fairly common occurrence. The other charges he lists are nonviolent and clearly revolve around being drunk, uncooperative, and homeless. Criminal trespassing is defined as entering someone's property and remaining there even though notice has been given that permission is not granted. The scenario would go something like this: Lonnie gets drunk and passes out on the grounds of a business (especially bad if it's one not licensed to serve liquor). The owner tells him to leave, but instead, Lonnie gets belligerent and uses abusive language. As the owner comes closer, Lonnie takes a swing at him with his cane. The owner calls the cops, Lonnie goes to jail, and he gets his private cell. When he is released the next morning, his first move is to relieve the shakes with a beer or two. On the day his court appearance is supposed to take place, he is asleep somewhere on someone else's property.

What he doesn't mention in his list of offenses is public urination. When I examined his rap sheet at the police station, this was among the most frequent charges. I know how disgusting this practice was. One Christmas, I was driving him to Mom's house when he asked me to stop at a convenience store so he could buy cigarettes. When he came out, he walked up to the car, opened the car door and, with his back to me and hidden from view by the door, urinated in the parking lot. There was a restroom in the convenience store—why couldn't he have used that? Too much trouble, he said, and he didn't want to get hassled by the owner. Because he looked filthy (and smelled worse), fast food restaurants, convenience stores, and other places where people might stop when they have to go to the bathroom were not available to him. So, he found spots where he could hide adequately. But at his worst, when he was drunk, he wasn't particular about whether he could be seen. The sight of a homeless man standing with his back to the street streaming into shrubbery or a garbage can is not uncommon. Depending on how careless the man was, he might find himself charged with indecent exposure, a much more serious offense. That never happened to Lonnie, but I don't doubt it could have.

How did he "evolve" into homelessness without noticing that he had no place to go to the bathroom?

5

August 1994

The worst place Lonnie had to sleep, by his earlier account, was in a homeless shelter. He hated being crowded among a lot of people, and he hated being inside if he could avoid it. Sleeping in the shelter of an elm cluster would be his ideal spot, especially one where no one could see him or reach him without waking him. But there was one hitch: bugs—biting ants and mosquitoes.

Bug spray was like gold. Lonnie reported getting mugged for his at least once, and he told me he considered it a sign of true friendship if someone was willing to share their bug repellent. In Houston (nicknamed the Bayou City), where the humidity is almost always high and standing water rarely evaporates completely, there are plenty of perfect breeding spots for mosquitoes. The spot Lonnie describes had security going for it, but a full night's sleep was impossible without bug spray, and with it, he might sleep *too* soundly, as he described on an earlier card, and wake up with his head on a log and missing his backpack—and his precious bug spray.

WHERE'S THE WORST PLACE YOU HAVE TO SLEEP?

BEHIND THE "HOLLYWOOD" CON-
VENCE STORE ON MONTROSE. THERE
IS A SHELTER OF SMALL ELMS.
I FIT IN THERE + NOBODY CAN
GET TO ME w/o WAKING ME.
THERE ARE ANTS + MOSQUITOES
♡ LJ

Card 62

Ants were less of a problem, because they could be dealt with through the use of a non-commercial repellent: urine. A free and plentiful supply was a big advantage for Lonnie. By dousing the ants, he both killed them and stopped the sting of their bites. Apparently when it dried, it worked as an effective deterrent to further assaults. Unfortunately, the mosquitoes were more determined and hardier, and were not fazed by ammonia or its smell.

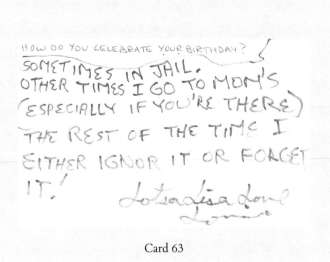

HOW DO YOU CELEBRATE YOUR BIRTHDAY?

SOMETIMES IN JAIL.
OTHER TIMES I GO TO MOM'S
(ESPECIALLY IF YOU'RE THERE)
THE REST OF THE TIME I
EITHER IGNOR IT OR FORGET
IT!
Lots a Lisa Love

Card 63

What answer was I expecting to this question? What answer was I hoping for? I'm sure I wished that someone would throw a party for him with presents and cake and candles. Birthdays were a big deal in our family. We always had presents and cake and candles, often a birthday party with our friends, and, in an era before Chuck E. Cheese and princess parties, they were always homespun. In addition, the birthday girl or boy got to choose the family's dinner menu. Lonnie's choice was usually fried chicken; mine was meatloaf. One year, Mom made my meatloaf in the shape of an owl—my birthday is close to Halloween—and meatloaf remained my annual choice right through adulthood. Most years, Mom insisted on making it in the shape of an owl.

As long as she had an address she could use for him, Mom always sent Lonnie a birthday card. (I sent them, too, but never as consistently as Mom.) If she could find a little gift to send, like some socks or a notebook, she wrapped it in birthday paper with a bow and packed it up in a manila envelope along with the card. Sometimes she sent him a little cash—no more than five or ten dollars, knowing what it would most likely be spent on, and also knowing that carrying any amount of cash could be dangerous for him.

When I wrote Lonnie this question, I'm sure I knew that the real answer was probably that he spent his birthday the way he spent any other day. "Sometimes in jail" was what I expected; "Other times I go to Mom's" was fictional. He would have been welcome at Mom's house if he was sober. But he would have to get there, traveling to the suburbs from Montrose. It was a three-bus transfer, a thirty-dollar cab ride or a who-knew-how-long hitchhike from Lonnie's corner to Mom's house in west Houston.

It wasn't something that could be done on the spur of the moment. Mom might be disinclined to open the door if she saw it was Lonnie and couldn't be sure he was sober. (She would then feel monumental guilt.) If she did open the door and he came in, how would he get back to his neighborhood? On one occasion, he caught a ride to her house with a friend who drove a cab. The friend and Lonnie walked up to the front door, and when Mom opened it, she realized immediately that she was about to be alone in the house with Lonnie and some guy she didn't know. She no doubt spent the whole time alternating between terror and guilt. First, she would be nervous—the cab driver might try to pull something, and Lonnie might not be able to protect her, or one or both of them would want money, and she wouldn't have any to give them. Then she would feel guilty for being nervous, and then she would cycle back to nervous, which, of course, was perfectly rational. Nothing happened, the guys proved pleasant enough company, and they left after an hour or two when Lonnie started to get the shakes.

There was another birthday, many years later, that went another

118 • Lisa Johnson

way. Lonnie called Mom before his birthday, hoping to connect to the solid reality of Mom's voice. He was sober when he called, and the chat was a long and lucid one. It ended with Lonnie saying he would like to come to the house on his birthday, and that Mom needn't worry, he would come on the bus. He couldn't say exactly when he would be able to get there, bus schedules being only approximate, but he would come in the afternoon. And, he assured her, he would be sober. She later told me she didn't really count on him showing up, since there were so many ways a plan with Lonnie could get derailed. But just in case he made it, she baked a birthday cake—pineapple upside-down cake, his favorite and one that she also liked and could enjoy with or without him. She ended up with the whole cake to herself. He called a few days later and explained that he couldn't get the bus fare together, and the bus schedule was messed up, and the cops jacked him up just before he was getting ready to leave for her house. This was the cost to Mom of Lonnie's lifestyle, and she paid it countless times. Her love for her son was indestructible.

My patience with him, on the other hand, was not limitless. Lonnie called Mom for a chat on Memorial Day weekend one year. He was sober and the conversation was, again, pleasant and cordial. Lonnie mentioned that he would like to go to the cemetery where his daughter and Dad are buried. Mom suggested they meet and asked him if he knew how to get there on the bus. He said he did. They set the time and agreed to meet at Dad's grave on Memorial Day.

The meeting time came and went, and Lonnie didn't show up. But Mom was smart—she had brought a book so she would have something to do in case Lonnie was late. Two hours passed, he still had not come, and Mom finally headed home. There was no call from Lonnie on her answering machine telling her why he couldn't make it, but several days later he called offering the same array of excuses he always gave. When Mom told me, she was philosophical about it—it was Lonnie, after all. But I was enraged. How could he treat Mom that way? Why was it always okay for Lonnie to be inconsiderate and selfish? Why did he always assume that he had the latitude to screw up? I wrote a letter to Lonnie in which I told him that yes, we loved him, and yes, we would always love him, but for crying out loud, Mom wasn't getting any younger, and there wouldn't always be opportunities for him to get together with her, and he owed her at least an apology.

The apology didn't come. In fact, Lonnie never even responded to the letter. I asked him a little later if he remembered the angry letter I had written him, and he said he remembered it but couldn't recall what I had said.

My resentment, built up over a lifetime of him getting second chances, had bubbled over. I was tired of being the good girl and him being the perpetual bad boy. I think that, as a little girl, I was well behaved because I was afraid if I didn't behave correctly, Mom and Daddy might not love me anymore. Why didn't that fear ever affect Lonnie? Maybe because in his half of our conjoined world, it never occurred to him that they expected anything else from him except bad behavior.

Maybe it was not alcoholism or mental illness that made him act like he was oblivious to everyone else's feelings. Maybe he really was oblivious. I can't be sure.

I don't remember ever being in Houston for Lonnie's birthday—I lived in Atlanta and traveled to Houston every Christmas, but by January 23, Lonnie's birthday, I would have been home and back at work. His comment about going to Mom's house "especially if you're there" was not so much a statement of fact as an oblique way of telling me how much he loved me. He ended the card with a sunny "Lotsa Lisa Love, Lonnie" written in script with a big, loopy "L" on each word.

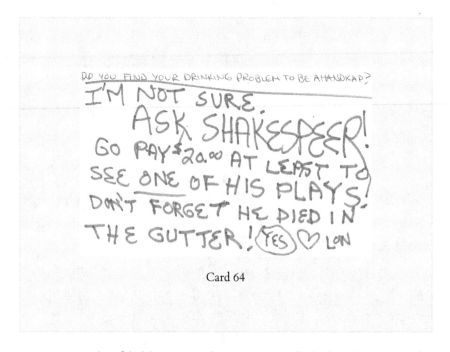

DO YOU FIND YOUR DRINKING PROBLEM TO BE A HANDICAP?

I'M NOT SURE.
ASK SHAKESPEER!
GO PAY $20.00 AT LEAST TO
SEE ONE OF HIS PLAYS!
DON'T FORGET HE DIED IN
THE GUTTER! (YES) ♡ LON

Card 64

Even to me this felt like a stupid question, and I believed I knew the answer. I wondered whether Lonnie's would match mine, but I was sure I wouldn't get a penitent "yes."

By way of an answer, he cites the case of William Shakespeare. He has the historical facts wrong—Shakespeare was fairly well off when he died. Lonnie has remade Shakespeare, casting him as a drunk, though one whose plays still command high ticket prices.

When his answer to my question comes, it is abrupt and clear: Yes. Shakespeare notwithstanding, Lonnie knew his drinking was a handicap. But he didn't elaborate, and I wish I had followed up. It was easy for me to see how it handicapped him physically. He was vulnerable to seizures any time he was overdue for a drink or a Dilantin. With alcohol taking priority over food, he was malnourished. His alcoholism likely contributed to the throat cancer that killed him.

It handicapped him in another, subtler way: Nobody could trust him or count on him. Alcohol is good as a social lubricant that facilitates parties, first dates, and after-hours business meetings. But for Lonnie, drinking created a defensive perimeter. It separated him from Mom pretty literally. It separated him from me because I was constantly wary, constantly assuming that nothing he said could be taken as fact.

I rarely let on to him that I didn't believe much of what he told me when he was drunk. In fact, I chided Mom for trying to parse out her conversations with Lonnie according to the rules of logic or rationality. I relied on "willing suspension of disbelief," conducting my own conversations with him in the same way as I might with Zorro or Olaf or Rick Dalton, teen detective. In the game of Imaginary Lonnie, my role was the credulous but intelligent and responsible sidekick. In other words, he did all the playing, I merely played along. I didn't much enjoy enabling his denial, but I knew trying to talk him back into reality was futile and risky. At risk was his willingness to have any sort of dialogue with me, fictitious or otherwise. Relating to this Imaginary Lonnie was better than having no Lonnie at all.

In his postcards, he was more grounded in reality than he typically was during face-to-face conversations, or even on the telephone. Face to face, his audience's reactions spurred him to greater heights of outrageousness, and on the phone, he was bound by not even a momentary look of disbelief from a listener. Writing the cards—maybe the act itself—had a significance for him that a transient conversation didn't. His writing on a piece of paper was tangible, undeniably real. I think he saw the cards as a chance to be known and remembered, and for the most part, he told the truth, or at least, his truth.

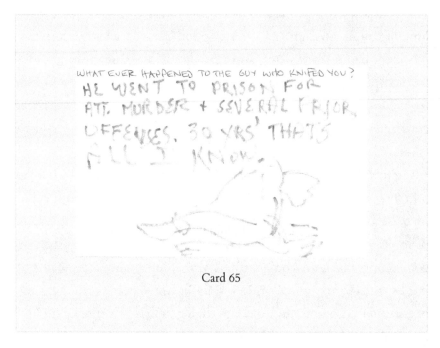

WHAT EVER HAPPENED TO THE GUY WHO KNIFED YOU?
HE WENT TO PRISON FOR
ATT. MURDER + SEVERAL PRIOR
OFFENCES. 30 YRS' THAT'S
ALL I KNOW.

Card 65

Whoever that knife-wielding man was, he was lucky it was my brother he attacked. Someone else with a weaker constitution would have died from the wounds and the blood loss—the emergency room doctor said so—and that would have meant a murder charge. Lonnie recovered in spite of more than a dozen wounds. Thus, his assailant was lucky.

Lonnie and I inherited what my Dad referred to as "good protoplasm." Ironically, we also inherited the cancer gene on Dad's side. Cancer killed Dad and three of his siblings and, ultimately, Lonnie, and I've had it twice. But Lonnie and I had resilient immune systems, and I wonder whether life on the street might have further strengthened Lonnie's. It's a theory so cockeyed that it is worthy of

Olaf himself: poor hygiene and worse nutrition, harsh weather, lack of medical care, the effects of alcohol and smoking—all the things that could have killed him, instead, taken together, may have provided an "extreme workout" that invigorated his antibodies. Lonnie survived somehow, his attacker went to prison, and Lonnie went his merry way. I know he loved that.

I don't know what the scribble is below the text on this card. It looks like an incomplete drawing, with what appears to be a leg stretched out to the left, and a wing on the right side. My guess is it's the beginning of a picture that Lonnie abruptly decided he no longer felt like drawing.

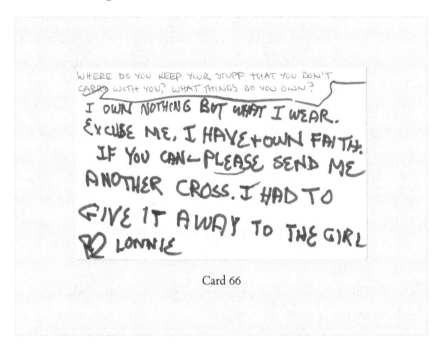

Card 66

Homeless people often walk around in the middle of summer wearing long, heavy coats over layers of sweatshirts. They don't have closets or dressers, garages or attics, spare rooms or junk drawers. They have pockets and their shoulders.

Lonnie didn't own much. He stashed a few clothes in his hiding places—an extra pair of jeans or a heavy jacket—but it was not exactly burdensome for him to carry everything he owned. It was harder later, when he was in a wheelchair, because he had to either sit on his possessions, hold them in his lap or carry them in a backpack he hung on the back of his chair. That was risky—the dangling backpack was virtually unprotected.

He said he owned faith and asked me to send him another cross. I had given him a small stone cross on a cord, something simple, not valuable, not immediately visible to a passerby. I figured he might actually be able to hold onto it. Instead, he "had to give it away." That was Lonnie's thinking. Maybe "the girl" gave him some sort of present, like a drawing, and he "had to" give her something in return. The cross would have been handy in his pocket or on a string around his neck.

"The girl" could have been the little girl who, a couple of cards from now, will be drawing with the colored pens I sent him. In a letter that I received a few days behind this set of cards, he called her a "little bitch" who stole his pens but closed the story with "ain't she cute." Lonnie quickly adopted children, and they were drawn to the kid they saw in him. It is not a big leap to say that, for whatever children crossed his path, he welcomed the chance to be "Daddy" in any way possible.

He had an impish side—small, teasing jokes and a mischievous giggle were his way of making you laugh. In his hospital bed, he might wear a bedpan as a helmet and salute you. On Christmas, he might take your brand-new ballerina doll and, while making it spin around in tiny pirouettes on top of a toy piano, sing ballet music in a squeaky high voice. Finally, he would collapse into giggles right along with you, both of you caught in a vortex of reciprocating laugh cycles. Lonnie's laugh was like Dad's. When he got going, it stopped coming out as "hahaha" or "heeheehee," and became a deep, wheezing "khkhkhkh" sound, while his face turned several shades of red and his eyes teared up.

True to his word, when Lonnie died and I went to the VA hospital to pick up his belongings, everything he owned fit into a small plastic grocery bag. There were a jacket and a pair of pants, the framed photo of Dad I had brought to his hospital room, a rhinestone watch, a small angel doll I had given him, a couple of notebooks, and two or three dollars in change.

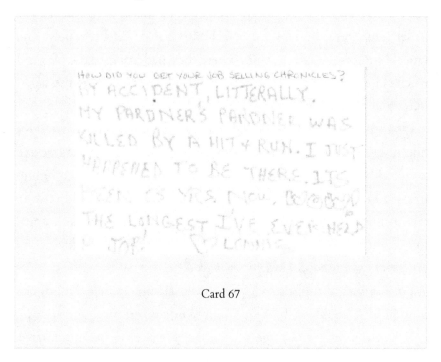

Card 67

Lonnie held the *Chronicle* job for three years, longer than any other job he had in his life. It had everything going for it: limited time commitment, friendly interaction with his regulars, and, best of all, it was outside. On the median of a busy street, the hazard of hit-and-run drivers was ever present. Lonnie was knocked out of this job by a pickup truck that jumped the curb, hit Lonnie, ran a red light and kept right on going. Once again, it was amazing he wasn't killed. Good protoplasm.

An ambulance took him to the VA hospital, where he was admitted right away, his leg was operated on, and he went through an enforced detox. Mom didn't find out he was in the hospital until he had been there for several days; she let me know as soon as she found out. I wanted to call him and tell him I was thinking of him, that I hoped he'd heal soon and be back on his feet. But there was one phone for the whole unit—10 or 15 beds—and even if someone answered, I could talk to Lonnie only if there was a nurse available to let him know he had a call, get him out of his bed safely, and wheel him to the visitors' room where they had installed the phone. I reached him once, I think, and the rest of the time I relayed messages, hugs, and kisses to him through Mom.

It was hard to be worried and angry at the same time. I hated for him to be hurt; I was furious that someone had hurt him and gotten away with it. I was mad at him for living a life that subjected him to this kind of horror, and for being in a place where I couldn't even talk to him on the phone. Yet I wanted him to stay in the hospital long enough to heal, and, more importantly, I wanted him there long enough to get sober and stay that way.

For Lonnie, it might as well have been prison. He left the hospital as soon as he could, with or without the doctor's recommendation.

When Lonnie was happiest (on the street and, in his mind, free), I was the most frustrated—without any way to call him, well aware of the hazards he faced, imagining what it would be like to have to scrounge for food or not to know where he was going to sleep at night. *I* couldn't have coped with scrounging. *I* couldn't have done without a safe, warm bed at night. In spite of what I consistently saw in his postcards, it was simply impossible for me to believe that Lonnie had the life he wanted, or that he could be content and at peace with himself. I had a hard time seeing him clearly in a reality that was so different from mine. If I had believed he was content and at peace with himself, I would have had to give up on him living some other way. I needed to hope that he might one day change his mind, and that when that time came, I somehow would be able help him move on. Hoping gave me purpose.

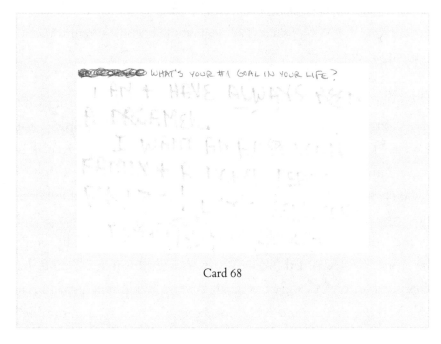

Card 68

I asked him what his goal was, and he told me his dreams. They were a lot like mine. He wanted an American family—Mom, Dad, two children, happy home, like the one he and I had as kids. He wanted a Nobel Peace Prize. Maybe he was thinking of a Nobel Prize for Literature, since he hurries to say, "Let's sell the BOOK!"

I am uneasy with goals. To set my life on the one, narrow path that will take me directly to the goal seems potentially oppressive.

If I don't take that fast, straight path (or, worse, if I wander away from it altogether), it's a character defect. People with goals often end up being driven by them. Driven is something I don't want to be. Motivated, inspired, committed, conscientious, diligent, passionate, yes—but not driven. Driven sounds obsessive. Books that have come out about the purpose-driven life, church, teen, or family are ominous to me—I don't want to be part of a family that is driven, by purpose or anything else. They would be snarly and competitive. They would be measuring each other constantly, the stronger ones prodding at the weaker ones. The goal would become tyrannical and, ultimately, destructive.

That's what I imagine, anyway.

I'm with Lonnie on this one. Dreams are positive, inspiring, and motivating. People with dreams are *drawn* forward, not driven. Of course, I know the aphorism about dreams, "a dream without a plan is just a wish." How about this: A goal without a dream is just a chore.

Look where all that dreaming got Lonnie and me. Lonnie never got to be a rock star. He never got to have the family he dreamed of, or the Nobel prize. The book will be finished, even though he won't be around to see it. I think he was fine with dreaming. I think he cherished his dreams almost as much as he would have if he had been able to bring them to reality. I think Lonnie's dreams *were* his reality, and a much more enjoyable reality than the one he lived in every day.

As for me, I didn't dream much past my 40s. When I was younger, I dreamed of a family, love, a rewarding and fulfilling career in advertising. My last dream (other than finishing and publishing this book) was a desire to be a pastor. I took the steps—seminary, denominational paperwork, and all the processes—but as it turned out, I wasn't that good at being a pastor, or at least not in the churches in which I tried my hand at it. I did fine in the pulpit, and in one-on-one ministry with my little "flocks." But church politics can be toxically present even in the smallest of churches, and they are what undid me. I mostly released that dream, even though for Lonnie it had come true and then some. He referred to me as "the Reverend Doctor Lisa Johnson," and, as I mentioned earlier, I was neither a reverend nor a doctor.

Lonnie's insistence on referring to me that way rankled me, being called by the title I had wanted so badly and that had eluded me. But Lonnie had ordained me and conferred a doctorate. My dream had come true in his reality.

Lonnie was content to dream his dreams and didn't see a reason to risk pain and disappointment trying to make them real. I had the wherewithal—education, health, and opportunity—to pursue dreams, but I didn't have any. Until, that is, Lonnie and I dreamed up this book, together.

As discussed on the next card, I'm sure Lonnie saw plenty of pregnant teenagers, what with Covenant House being a couple of blocks away from his corner. Maybe the girl on this card is a composite of all of them, or maybe she is the most recent he has seen. The baby is a boy, the ultrasound designates, and the girl is keeping him. Thumbs up. But, Lonnie adds, she will have problems. She will most likely have to raise him alone. She will have to figure out how to find and keep a job, and how to provide for the baby's care while she works or goes to school. Lonnie is uncharacteristically realistic.

YOU MENTIONED A 13-YR-OLD PREGNANT GIRL, DID SHE
HAVE HER BABY YET? WHAT WILL HAPPEN TO THE BABY?
O.K. LITTLE PINK—
SHE IS VERY CLOSE NOW,
BUT NOT QUIET! ULTRASOUND
DESIGNATES A BOY. SHE IS
KEEPING HIM ☞ THUMBS UP
P.S. SHE WILL HAVE PROBLEMS
LJ

Card 69

Maybe he is remembering what it felt like to become a parent, how heavy the burdens of responsibility were, even to a 24-year-old man with a loving spouse. He adored his daughter, played with her, cuddled her. But he found it hard to be a father and husband. He and his wife split up when their daughter was less than two years old. On several of his postcards, Lonnie said he wished he could have another chance to be a daddy.

I barely got to know Tookie before she died. I lived in New York at the time, and I was in college and going through a legal separation from my husband. When my parents needed to tell me that the baby had died, they called my husband and asked him to come to my apartment and tell me in person so I wouldn't be left alone with the devastating news.

I was about 21 years old, and, with the end of my marriage and my immersion in college life, my own prospects for parenthood had receded. But I wasn't thinking about that, I was thinking about school and dating and my part-time job at a jewelry store. It didn't occur to me that I might end up childless, that losing my niece meant losing the closest thing I would ever have to a child of my own.

I didn't go to the funeral. I can't say why. I can't even imagine why. I don't like to think how it must have felt to Lonnie that I wasn't there for him. Maybe I didn't want to acknowledge Tookie's death so definitively. It took me several years before I could visit her gravesite, and it is still difficult and unnerving.

Little Pink, he called me, and he wrote the card entirely in pink ink, a tribute to the brave teen mother-to-be, to Lonnie's daughter and her mother, to me. I didn't deserve the tribute. At 13, I wouldn't have been brave enough to keep a baby. At 13, I didn't even know where they came from.

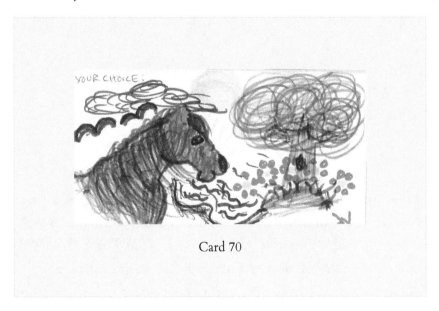

Card 70

Suddenly Lonnie had his little girl back. The girl he mentioned earlier, who showed up wearing his backpack one morning, is apparently the artist who "stole" his pens. I gave him his choice of topics on this card, and he turned the card over to the little girl for her artwork.

It's sunny where she is, with chunky flowers next to a clear, blue stream, and her horse with its mischievous eye and its silky black mane blowing in the breeze. Her drawing reminds me of the picture Lonnie drew of the long-haired woman sitting under a tree.

IF YOU COULD GO BACK AND DO SOMETHING DIFFERENTLY, WHAT WOULD IT BE? I SHOULD HAVE STAYED w/ MOUSE + TOOKIE! THEY LOVED ME SO MUCH! I ALSO SHOULD HAVE STAYED w/ MY MUSIC. IT WAS A GIFT FROM GOD + I PAWNED IT! ♡ LNJ

Card 71

Mouse and Tookie loved him so much. This is one big what-if. If he had stayed with them, would he have avoided alcoholism? Would he have been able to pursue a music career? Would he have had the family he dreamed of, the familiar, steady life we grew up with?

Our stories converge in uncomfortable places in my life, unresolved places. I should have stayed with my husband, who loved me so much. I would have lived an entirely different life. I would have had children.

Lonnie stayed with his music as long as he could. In the end, he had very little voice left and almost no mobility in the hands that had grown up wrapped around the neck of a guitar. But for many years, he could make a little money by playing a borrowed guitar and setting a hat out on the sidewalk to collect donations.

Lonnie's musical gifts were considerable. He could pick up and play any instrument. He could listen to a piece of music and duplicate the melody on a piano or pick out the chords on a guitar. He had a rough but perfectly on-key singing voice, until smoking and alcohol took away his breath. He was in several rock-and-roll bands as a teenager, to my starry-eyed delight. He found fellow musicians when he was in the Army. When he was in Texas State Prison in Huntsville, he was part of the prison band. They were good enough to play at the Texas Prison Rodeo. Not surprisingly, Lonnie said it was the best part of the time he spent in prison.

What happened to his music? He sang and played guitar with Mouse (they met at a recording studio). He worked as a studio musician at times over the years. He set a Guinness Book record for one-man band, playing three or more instruments for nearly 18 hours in a bar in Montrose. Eventually, he could neither sing nor play with the same skill, and once he was on the street, he couldn't hang onto a guitar long enough to use it as a tool for making money.

He pawned his music, he says. It was a gift from God, and he pawned it. I don't know why he thought that. I think he simply lost it. He smoked and drank and lived a brutal, physically taxing life, and he lost his music. When you pawn something, you get money for it.

This comment has always seemed a better fit for my life than for Lonnie's. My writing is a gift from God, too. I used it and practiced my craft, but I decided to cash in on it, for what seemed like a lot of money at the time, by working in the advertising business. The message on this card has always stirred a bit of guilt in me, and as I work on this book, it speaks to me again. This project is not pawning my writing. This project is using it for good purpose, unlike selling it to an employer in exchange for writing what I am told. With this book, I feel like I am redeeming my pawn ticket.

6

November 1994

Three months went by between card 71 and card 72. My asking him if it was okay to send more stuff indicates that he was not available to retrieve it for some reason that I knew at the time but have since forgotten. The possibilities are few—hospital or jail.

well? Can I send you more stuff?
I'VE ONLY GOT 1 LITTLE SISTER!
NO ONE ELSE WILL DO!
I SHED HAPPY TEARS
           CAUSE YOU LOVE ME
AND I HOPE YOU KNOW
      I LOVE U!
TO ANSWER YOUR ? GO TO A RE-
SALE SHOP, GET A CHEAP SMALL
BACK PACK & LOAD IT W/CARDS!

Card 72

I was working at an ad agency where my job was demanding but fun, and I was making good money. Two years had passed since my cancer diagnosis. I was over the worst of the chemotherapy side effects, but deep into hot flashes and weight issues. Drifting through my mind was the obstinate idea of becoming a pastor, going to seminary and being ordained, and I was making my way through the denomination's rigorous, structured process of discerning the meaning of that persistent restlessness.

My relationship with Lonnie anchored me. I had the job, income, home—proven competency at life. He had . . . none of that—proven incompetency at life. We were still the bad boy and the good girl by most outside estimates. But I was closing in on ditching my career in advertising and replacing it with work that could be expected to pay at best half as much (less for a beginner). I'm sure Mom slapped her forehead regularly and wondered what might be wrong with her usually lucid daughter. I knew she loved me and would support me whatever I decided, and later, she became deeply proud of her pastor daughter. But I also knew she had misgivings about my future, especially financially, and especially in comparison to the income I enjoyed in advertising.

Lonnie was rock solid. He loved me, he looked up to me, he believed in me. He didn't question anything I did or thought about or wanted. He just accepted me, and he was as comfortable as I was in our closed system. He didn't want to be the competent one. I'm not sure I wanted to either, but I was already good at it, and it was my default role.

He wrote me a poem, or a song, on this card. It's sentimental and sunny; Lonnie in his cheerful, innocent world. At one time when we were very young, we pretended to be Cubby and Karen, two of the first Mouseketeers on the original 1950s Mickey Mouse Club TV show. They were the youngest, the most playful and mischievous. The poem was written by Cubby-Lonnie, in a world where he loves me, and I love him and that's all he needs to know.

His answer to my "?" was that of a street-smart man talking to his younger, less savvy sister (whom he loved all the same). "Go to a resale shop" (not a sporting goods store) "and get a cheap" (not attractive to thieves), "small" (inconspicuous) "backpack and load it with cards!"

I didn't want to send him too many cards at once because I didn't want to risk losing more than five or six cards at a time. I enjoyed making up the questions. They started out focused on simple logistics—where he slept, how he got food—but my curiosity about who he was deepened with every card, and I started asking more challenging, more personal questions. He liked them. It tickled him that *I* might be interested in these details about him and his life, and even more that I thought other people might want to read about him.

WHAT DID YOU LEARN IN SCHOOL THAT YOU USE ON THE STREET? EASY! — POSITIVE + NEGATIVE REINFORCE-MENT THIS IS AMAZING! WHAT I KNOW IS WHAT I DO! YOU WOULD BE SURPPISED! I ENJOY MY LITTLE SISTER, AND I AM AN ASS-HOLE! BUT I LOVE YOU

Card 73

I don't know what answer I expected—geometry? The state capitals? Iambic pentameter? I'm surprised Lonnie didn't answer with tongue planted firmly in cheek.

If he learned positive and negative reinforcement in school, he learned it not in a classroom but by experiencing many rounds of discipline in a variety of forms. He surely knew what had worked on him and what hadn't. I struggle to imagine that anything at all worked on him. I can be pretty confident in saying that negative reinforcement had zero impact. But positive reinforcement is another question. When would he have experienced it? From the time he started misbehaving, his rewardable behavior started to dwindle. Besides, the role of good child belonged firmly and irreversibly to me.

I got plenty of positive reinforcement, and I came to be as deeply addicted to it as Lonnie later was to alcohol. As with substance addiction, my craving for approval, and the dose I needed to satisfy it fully, grew exponentially. My high grades in school were the clearest and most accessible form of applause, since school was pretty easy for me (as it would have been for Lonnie, if he had "applied himself"). Grades set specific, defined parameters. I got used to someone else setting my goals, and to the reliable outcomes I knew I could count on when I achieved them. In addition to grades, I got endless praise and encouragement from Mom and Dad. I doubt they ever told Lonnie they wished he were an achiever like me, though I imagine they quietly wished it at times. I'm sure Lonnie assumed they wished it.

He may have despaired of ever catching up to the stockpile of "good" I had amassed, especially in school, and decided it wasn't worth it to try. So, he took his own direction: How little can I do and still get by? His teachers were onto him, of course, which is obvious in their comments on his early report cards: "Lonnie would be such a good student if he would only . . ." What they didn't grasp about him was that he had no intention of shooting for "good student." He applied his brains and imagination to carving out his own role, and it had everything to do with being not-the-good-one.

Maybe I give our symbiosis too much credit. I can only talk definitively about my side of it, but from over here, who I was and who Lonnie was were mutually defining. I wonder what would have happened to our relationship, for example, if a miracle had occurred and Lonnie had suddenly found his way into sobriety, a job, a home, and a family. I suspect I would have been out to sea, along with Mom and, in earlier years, Dad. Our family dynamic was built around Lonnie, just as, after Dad died, Mom's and my Christmases revolved around Lonnie—getting him to the house, figuring out what to serve that he could eat with no teeth, keeping him sober enough to be sane but not so sober that he had a seizure. Lonnie wasn't the unacknowledged elephant in the room, he was the elephant ruling the room.

Lonnie closes this card by reminding me that he is an asshole, "*but*," he says, "I love you." "I am the bad one, don't forget"—the message and the language of the message are unmistakable misbehaviors. But he still loves his little sister.

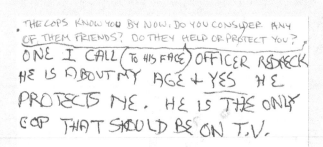

, THE COPS KNOW YOU BY NOW, DO YOU CONSIDER ANY
OF THEM FRIENDS? DO THEY HELP OR PROTECT YOU? ,
ONE I CALL (TO HIS FACE) OFFICER REDNECK
HE IS ABOUT MY AGE + YES HE
PROTECTS ME. HE IS THE ONLY
COP THAT SHOULD BE ON T.V.

Card 74

The police in the Montrose storefront location knew Lonnie from the dozens of times they had responded to complaints against him, and from the many calls for an ambulance when he had a seizure or was mugged or got clobbered while being shooed away from some doorway or dumpster. The emergency calls to Mom never came from the police but always from the hospital (if they came at all, which depended on how lucid Lonnie was when he was brought in).

Lonnie's relationship with the police was not entirely adversarial. They tolerated the little scams he pulled to get locked up on nights when the cold or heat or rain or mosquitoes were unbearable. They arrested him dozens of times for public intoxication, public urination, trespassing, resisting arrest, and whatever it's called when a drunk guy mouths off once too often to a put-upon officer. But Lonnie admitted that Officer Redneck protected him, which probably meant that from time to time, somebody who was threatening Lonnie got hauled away in handcuffs. He "should be on TV"—that acclamation put Officer Redneck in impressive company. The TV cops Lonnie and I grew up with were tough, compassionate, no-nonsense men (always men): Sgt. Joe Friday ("Dragnet"), Lt. Philip Gerard ("The Fugitive") and Chief Dan Mathews ("Highway Patrol"). They were heroes, and for Lonnie to place Officer Redneck in their class was rare and revealing.

For Mom and me, the police station was the one sane place we could go when we were desperate for information about Lonnie. This only happened when I came home for a visit and we hadn't heard from him, leaving us with no way to arrange a get-together. Sometimes I drove down to Westheimer and Montrose and scanned the neighborhood, looking in all his places. If I didn't find him, and if none of the "regulars" had seen him recently, I went to the police station to inquire. I knew they would tell me if they knew where he was, which meant the hospital (they would have called the ambulance) or in jail. At the least, they would tell me when they had seen him last, and what shape he had been in at that time.

On one visit to the storefront, I asked if I could see Lonnie's rap sheet. The officer excused himself and disappeared into the back offices. When he came out several minutes later, he was carrying a computer printout, the old kind where the sheets were connected to each other. Unfolded, it was about seven feet long. "Oh, yeah," the officer sighed, "we all know Mr. Johnson quite well." *Mr.* Johnson.

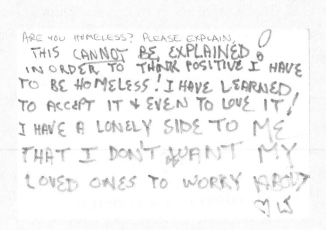

ARE YOU HOMELESS? PLEASE EXPLAIN.
THIS CANNOT BE EXPLAINED
IN ORDER TO THINK POSITIVE I HAVE
TO BE HOMELESS! I HAVE LEARNED
TO ACCEPT IT & EVEN TO LOVE IT!
I HAVE A LONELY SIDE TO ME
THAT I DON'T WANT MY
LOVED ONES TO WORRY ABOUT
♡ LJ

Card 75

Mom worked hard at not worrying about Lonnie. She was not entirely successful, of course. She worried he would get mugged, or forget to take his Dilantin, or stumble drunk into the path of an oncoming bus. She worried that some mosquito would give him the West Nile virus, or he would get food poisoning, or be shot by some irate store owner. She worried that he might get depressed and commit suicide or become addicted to God knew what. There were a thousand things to worry about, but I don't know that Mom or Dad or I ever considered worrying about Lonnie being lonely.

For one thing, we all saw him as the charming, popular kid he always had been, the handsome boy who could smile and crack a joke and instantly have a new friend. I was envious of that gift. It seemed like Lonnie was set for life with his personality and good looks. When I once went to the Covenant House near Lonnie's corner to talk to a staff member whom Lonnie had mentioned, she immediately knew who Lonnie was: the older guy with the "beautiful blue eyes," she said. In fact, I was able to contact a friend of Lonnie's from junior high—more than 50 years ago—who remembered his "great hair and intense blue eyes."

Lonnie had made plenty of friends on the street, but they were the kind that came and went with his supply of cash, bug spray, cigarettes, matches, beer or, at Christmas and on his birthday, socks. Mom was his rock. Anytime he could stay sober and dig up enough money to make a call from a pay phone, he could count on her for his one and only reliable connection to his real life, and to his history. She also provided the connection between Lonnie and me, but it was a tenuous one. I was far away, and besides, Mom could forge a connection only after Lonnie checked in to hear my news and relay his own. The postcards that started this book were the first steady, direct communication Lonnie and I had had in years.

He had a kind of social circuit, apart from the street people who clustered on the same corners he inhabited. There were waitresses, laundromat attendants, bartenders, and the rare shopkeepers who tolerated him, such as the flower shop owner who let us use the shop's address and allowed Lonnie to come around to get his mail. There were a couple of homeless services organizations—Star of Hope and SEARCH—where he received help enough times for his face and name to be known, and for him to know some faces and names, too. A few of the nurses, doctors, and social workers at the VA hospital knew him from his seizures, detoxes, and various injuries and chronic illnesses.

As I write this, I am overweight. But I was not always overweight. I was once a tennis player, a hiker, and a shortstop on my girls' softball team. I jogged every day, 4-6 miles, and even claimed a hard-won bronze medal in one 5K race (third place in my age class, out of four contenders, on a February day with single-digit temperatures). I sometimes feel alienated from people who have never known me as anything but overweight, because they know only the heavy woman who obscures the me that I know.

Maybe Lonnie was lonely not because he didn't have any friends, but because none of his friends knew the Lonnie that he knew.

HI LEETSAI,
I SURE LOVED YESTERDAY.
I SUPPOSE YOU'RE GONE
BY NOW. THE NIGHT WAS
PEACEFUL + TODAY IS
GOING AS PLANNED.
I'M WAITING ON THE
BUS + DECIDED TO TRY
OUT ONE OF THESE CARDS.
I DON'T HAVE ANYTHING
HARD TO WRITE ON
BUT MY HEAD, + IF I DO
THAT I CAN'T SEE WHAT
I'M WRITING, SO I
FORGIVE THE SLOP.
I'LL WRITE LOTS LATER!
7/ERES THE BUT HOLE
BUS! I LOVE YA
YO' BRUDDA

Card 76

There are no other cards that are written in blue ballpoint ink in neat, all-capital letters. I may have lost the other cards in this set, or else Lonnie wrote this one by itself and then wrote the others in another frame of mind. There is no postmark to date the card, but Lonnie said he "loved yesterday," so he was writing the day after we connected for a visit—at Christmas, most likely. His grammar and handwriting look sober, and his thinking is orderly. He reported that the day was "going as planned."

"Leetsai" is a name I made up for myself as a little girl. This nickname matched the names I made up for Lonnie, Mom and Dad: Lonsai, Mudsai and Fodsai. I have no idea where these names came from, but they were not the first words I had made up. Lonnie was always willing to go along with my language, and even though our parents probably wondered at times whether there was something wrong with me, they played along, too. There was the "Lop-o-ton song," which I wrote about in an earlier chapter. There was the phrase "dawdlin' crawn." "Dawdlin'" (it never had a "g" on the end) was, of course, a real word. "Crawn" was a term I created to designate someone silly or goofy. It was affectionate, not derogatory, but paired with "dawdlin'," it was a mild form of teasing. "Contince" meant likable or adorable (a doll might be "contince"). These were words distinct from baby talk, although the baby words "reraff" (giraffe), "halloweenie bean dip" (jalapeño bean dip), and "nannos" (bananas) were part of our family lexicon, too. I claimed words as my medium early on, but even as a child I preferred to use them in nonfiction settings, not, as Lonnie did, in acts of imagination.

There was no question on this card to direct Lonnie's choice of subject matter, so he chose to make me laugh, complaining that the only available hard surface to write on was his head, and if he used that, he wouldn't be able to see what he was writing. This was Lonnie's sense of humor—self-deprecating, goofy, imaginative. Our family did a lot of laughing together. Each of us had a robust sense of humor, and we were always eager to laugh at each other's gags.

There were running gags, like Dad putting Trappey's hot sauce on everything from corn bread to mashed potatoes to carrots. He would eat pepper sauce—or sliced jalapeño peppers—until his face turned red and he started to sweat. The joke became offering him the hot sauce at the most inappropriate times—for his pancakes, say, in his coffee, or on a slice of pumpkin pie. He enjoyed taking the bottle and, straight-faced, sprinkling hot sauce over whatever ridiculous thing we had dared him to anoint, then tucking into it with a big smile and much smacking of his lips. The gag was that, even as he was proclaiming the innovation delicious, his eyes were bugging out and he was flushing vividly.

Lonnie and I had a lot of running gags. Fighting over the duck skin at Thanksgiving or Christmas was one. It was greasy and crisp, and both of us considered it a treat, so we invented ways to finagle each other out of the even shares Mom tried to parcel out. We made bets, double-dog dared, actually hid the pieces of skin, and loomed over the oven waiting to pounce as soon as the duck came out. On the other hand, we always traded hated foods under the table. Lonnie took my Brussels sprouts; I took his peas. We both mock retched over the anchovies Mom and Dad treasured on pizza, policing the line between their half of the pizza and ours with fanatical thoroughness.

In a prayer I wrote for one of our last family Thanksgivings, I thanked God for all the lines on all our faces—laugh lines, mostly, that showed our lifelong dedication to horsing around with each other.

7

January/February 1998

What a week. An argument with my boss, a missed deadline, an overdue electric bill. No damage to me.

If Lonnie says one fight was a win and the other debatable, debatable probably translated into a pummeling. "Debatable" is the closest he could come to admitting he'd lost a fight. A rip-off meant someone knocked him down and took his backpack or his wheelchair or helped themselves to his stuff while he was asleep or passed out, or came across it stashed on a roof or in a hedge and grabbed it. He ended any speculation by testifying that there was no damage to him—another installment in his "don't worry about me" messages.

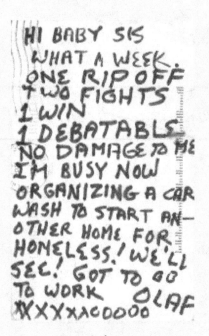

Card 77

At some point, I stopped worrying. I didn't stop thinking about him or wondering how he was getting along, especially if the weather was cold or rainy or super hot. But worrying was pointless; it was groundless, according to Lonnie. He could transform into a junkyard dog if backed into a corner. His self-defense instincts kicked in, along with his Army training, his football skills, and every surviving shred of machismo. He never accepted victimhood. It would have horrified him to think of himself that way, let alone have his mama or his "baby sis" think it.

I knew that a lot of what Lonnie told Mom and me, including his confidence in his ability to take care of himself, was wishful thinking. On the other hand, both of us had dealt with Lonnie when he was drunk. The aggressive persistence he turned loose at those times, together with his ability to reject self-governing, provided an effective and accessible arsenal I believed he could tap into at will. Even though I was pretty sure he would never actually hurt me, I still found him scary and truly menacing when he was drunk and angry, like the day I wouldn't let him into Mom's house because I could smell alcohol on his breath.

On this card, after dispelling all fear with his four-word declaration—"No damage to me"—Lonnie took a 180-degree turn away from the terrible week he was having. The car wash idea appeared out of nowhere and vanished just as abruptly; he never mentioned it again in the cards or on the phone. It's possible he was actually involved in some sort of community project between drinking bouts. But as loathsome as he found homeless shelters, I can't see him throwing himself into building one. Instead, I suspect he thought of the most benign image he could and inserted himself into it. He knew it would work for me, because at the time I was in my second year of seminary and, as part of my training, was working at a homeless shelter/soup kitchen one day a week.

It was a hard assignment, but not for the reasons I would have expected. In fact, it was almost the opposite—I found myself nearly unable to listen sympathetically to the guests' stories, knowing from experience that they were mostly fabrications. Then, feeling guilty for stereotyping homeless people, I returned to listening avidly until I heard a triggering phrase, like mentioning a pregnant teenager whose baby they had delivered. Lonnie had delivered his pregnant teenager's baby many times over the years, and, combined with other reasons I struggled to believe his stories, I was equipped with a wide streak of skepticism. One of my classmates saw it differently. He referred to my skepticism as a "crap detector," and suggested that my ability not to be taken in would make me better able to relate to homeless people and more likely to get them to communicate honestly with me. I didn't buy it. I hoped to gain insight into my brother but discovered that instead, I heard the same kind of patter I often heard from him.

There was one young man, Frederick, with whom I think I managed to establish an authentic relationship—as authentic as it could be with only one hour for conversation each week. I called him on his familiar stories of rotten bosses and lost jobs, of big opportunities he had missed because nobody would give him bus fare. He laughed with me when he was caught, and soon stopped trying to put one over on me. We began to have conversations. We talked about the day's headlines and about our families. We talked about his recovery from alcoholism and my struggle with weight issues. We prayed together, and for each other. Eventually, I let him persuade me to help him find an apartment. I was wise (or skeptical) enough not to give him money or any other material support, but I did give him a ride to a job interview, and, later, to an apartment complex to tour an apartment he thought he could afford. He showed up punctually both times and met me at the agreed upon spot. I waited in the car while he conducted his business, and he emerged with paperwork that he proudly shared with me. Within a few weeks, he stopped coming to the soup kitchen, and I never saw him again. I decided that his job interview had been a success, he had signed a lease, and he no longer needed to eat at a soup kitchen. I struggled to believe it.

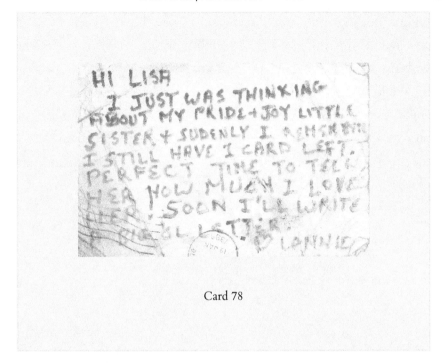

Card 78

Lonnie didn't place expectations on me, or criticize me, or expect me to be someone I wasn't. He told me dozens of times that I was his pride and joy. He introduced me to his friends that way—"This is my little sister, my pride and joy, the Reverend Doctor Lisa Johnson." A couple of them told me that he bragged about me a lot, and that they felt they knew me.

Okay, so he loved a reinvented version of me, a larger-than-life Little Pink who had achieved everything she (and he) had ever dreamed of. But for him, that's who I was, not who he wished I was or who he hoped I might one day become.

I wondered, even then, why he took such pride in my accomplishments—education, a career, a car, a place to sleep where I wouldn't get rained on. He seemed to put so little stock in such things for himself. After a certain point, I suppose he simply chose to leave accomplishment to me. He was able to applaud and admire mine without feeling jealous or threatened. I knew he loved me without any agenda, unconditionally. I couldn't say the same. I loved him with my whole heart, but I never, to the end, let go of the hope that he would be able to change his life—to be sober, to have an address and a phone number. I was not as good at accepting our two lives as he was. Or, he saw more clearly that our lives were a paired set, as they had always been, and didn't need to change. He accepted both of us as we were. I did not. I wish I had.

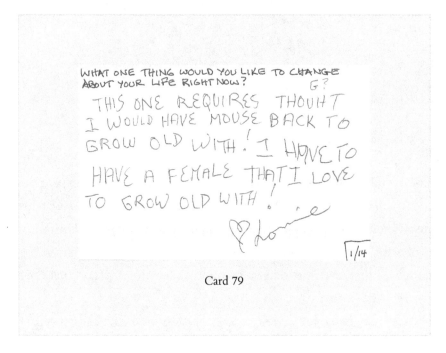

Card 79

He wanted what I still want, what everyone wants, what is made explicit in wedding vows—someone to share the years that are not so glamorous, or prosperous, or adventuresome. There is a scene at the end of the movie "Driving Miss Daisy," in which the aged matron is in a nursing home and her former chauffeur, Hoke, visits her. She is finishing her meal, ready for her slice of pumpkin pie for dessert, but her hand is too shaky to get the fork to her mouth. Hoke notices and tenderly cuts the bites and feeds her the pie. She gazes at him, the truest friend she ever had, with complete trust. Just thinking about that scene makes me well up. Who will feed me my pie?

Lonnie had, and lost, two wives. Magda stayed in touch with Mom, never failing to ask how Lonnie was doing. When Lonnie died, she sent us a card. I wish they had stayed together, too, for his reasons and my own: She might have provided the stability and strength he needed to get sober and get his life under control. She was Tookie's mother, and they could have helped each other to hold the memory of their child.

Lonnie's second wife was much younger than he and seemed more of a girlfriend than a wife. They were in love, I believe, in a way. But it didn't last, in part because her parents were not thrilled with her choice of husbands. I couldn't blame them. By the time she and Lonnie were marrying, Lonnie was far down the road to alcoholism, and his livelihood depended on playing music, mostly in bars. He never mentioned her in any of the cards. When he was remembering and longing, it was always for Mouse and Tookie.

WHAT IS THE BIGGEST DANGER TO YOU ?

LONLINESS

1/14/98

Card 80

This is one of the few answers that caught me completely off-guard. When I asked Lonnie about the biggest danger, I had in mind disease, cold, heat, hunger, seizures, or being shot, knifed, beat up, or run over. Loneliness never entered my mind. How was loneliness a danger to Lonnie? A burden, a trial, a pain—but how was it a danger?

Loneliness could lead a person to think about suicide. Lonnie occasionally expressed a sense of fatigue, a glum wish that he could get off the street. But he never indicated any interest in suicide. That doesn't mean he never thought of it. But he wouldn't express it where his loved ones could hear it—he would have been determined to protect us. On this card, though, he didn't offer any disclaimer about not worrying, or "no damage to me."

Loneliness could have made Lonnie disappear completely into alcohol—that was a real danger. I'm not sure whether he knew when to stop drinking, or just relied on his body to set the limit by passing out when he reached capacity. I know that's how alcohol works with non-alcoholics, but Lonnie's relationship with alcohol was complicated. He stayed at some level of drunk virtually all the time, except when he was taking Dilantin to prevent seizures. At Mom's house for Christmas Day, he could drink a six-pack of light beer without showing the slightest sign of intoxication, but it provided enough alcohol to keep him from seizing.

Loneliness presented a greater and more personalized danger for Lonnie. He defined himself by relationships. As a kid, he was good at making friends, and he was always surrounded by boys and girls who loved being around him. On the street, he had his "pride." He talked about the kids at the Covenant House, for whom he saw himself in the role of a trusted counselor. To be lonely would be to lose the one ability he relied on to provide his sense of belonging or connection. It would be to lose his sense of himself.

This is the only time Lonnie gave me a one-word answer. It was misspelled and a little shaky, but it was emphatic.

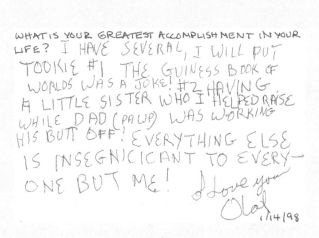

Card 81

He says he had many accomplishments. I can think of several, although they might not be the ones he had in mind: the many times he was able to go long periods of time without any alcohol, earning his GED, winning a marksmanship medal in Army basic training, and being (in my eyes, anyway) a rock star. It was an achievement of a kind for him simply to survive from day to day. I agree with him, though, that his daughter was his No. 1 achievement, in the sense that she was a lively, bright, loving little girl. She was his very own Little Pink, and that connection is clear in what he chooses as his second achievement: helping raise me "while Pawp was working his butt off."

While we lived in Atlanta and especially after we moved to Topeka, Dad was out of town more than he was at home. During Dad's absences, Lonnie was the "man of the house," a phrase I'm sure Dad spoke to Lonnie more than once. But I can't imagine that Dad believed it for a moment, or that he had any illusions that Mom and I would rely on Lonnie in that capacity. By the time we lived in Topeka, Lonnie, now in high school, was gone at least as much as Dad was, and Lonnie's departures and arrivals were completely unpredictable. We always knew when Dad was going to get home, and he called us every night to check in, updating us if there had been a change in his plans. Lonnie, on the other hand, crawled out into the night through his basement window well and might not crawl back in for several days. He was gone for a full week once without a phone call, while Mom and Dad desperately called the parents of his friends, the high school, his coaches—whoever might have an inkling where he was.

Still, I remember times when Mom and Dad went out for the evening and left me in Lonnie's care. I found this alarming even then, and now it seems downright dangerous. Of course, those were different times. But Lonnie was not always the diligent caregiver they paid him to be. He liked to have his girlfriends over while Mom and Dad weren't home. I don't know what else might have gone on during those trysts, but I caught him entangled on the couch more than once, and on occasion I remember thinking his breath smelled funny—alcohol, though at the time I didn't know that's what it was.

I took full financial advantage of Lonnie's babysitting occasions. What he didn't know was that Mom and Dad paid *me*, too. I guess they realized it might be a trying experience for me. I doubled my income by blackmailing Lonnie. When he realized I had caught him "on the couch," he always begged me not to tell Mom and Dad. Even a 10-year-old can see when she's got leverage.

What Lonnie didn't know (I hope I enlightened him later on) is that his role in raising me was more significant than he knew. He taught me how to imagine. He taught me adventure. He taught me rebellion. And when I say, "he taught me," I mean he did it, and I watched and learned. I am a brave person, and I think the image of myself as a Viking warrior or a teen detective had something to do with that.

He put music in my hands when he taught me how to play the guitar. He showed me four chords by letting me hold his precious electric guitar and finger the chords until I learned them. I got my hands on a guitar book and learned more, until I knew enough to play most songs I liked. Later, I wrote songs of my own and performed in a few small venues. I even had one song recorded by a famous group. I still play occasionally, and I still love the sound of a guitar.

Poor old Mr. Case, my childhood piano teacher, never ignited the fire that my rock star big brother did with those four chords.

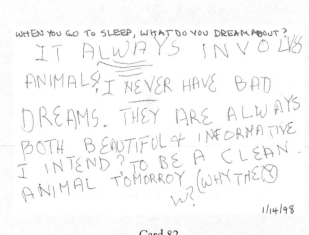

WHEN YOU GO TO SLEEP, WHAT DO YOU DREAM ABOUT? IT ALWAYS INVOLVS ANIMALS! I NEVER HAVE BAD DREAMS. THEY ARE ALWAYS BOTH BEAUTIFUL & INFORMATIVE I INTEND? TO BE A CLEAN - ANIMAL TOMORROY (WHY THE) W? 1/14/98

Card 82

Lonnie told me that, during one of his longer stays in the detox program, he had worked at the VA hospital in the research lab, taking care of the animals. He talked about dogs and mice and monkeys, what fun it was to groom them and feed them, and how he liked to sneak one or two out of their cages to play with them. This lab and the job may be fictional. But Lonnie's affinity for animals runs throughout his cards, from "Soc the Mog" to the "peaceful and reassuring" pigeons to his remembered (or imagined) work with the lab animals.

We didn't have a lot of pets growing up. I got a cat for Christmas when I was 8 or 9 years old—Prissy, an all-black Persian mix. I adored her, but she wasn't much of a lap kitty, so none of us formed an intense bond with her. When I was in high school, a friend brought a tiny Dachshund puppy to my house. He had found it wandering around the high school, he said, and wondered if I would like to keep it. I liked this boy a lot, so I agreed to keep the puppy, at least for a while, until he could find it a permanent home. Missy was so smart and cute that she quickly found her own permanent home with us, and the cat came to terms with the intruder, dealing with the dog mostly by ignoring her.

That was it for pets in our family. When we got Missy, Lonnie was still in Kansas at the Menninger Clinic while Mom, Dad, and I had moved to Houston, so he barely knew her. I don't know where his fondness for animals came from, but I could speculate. Animals don't ask you if you filled out this or that form. They don't ask how many days it's been since your last drink, or make you pee in a cup to make sure you're telling the truth. They don't tell you to get a haircut or take a shower. Animals bond and trust and depend on you unconditionally. They love unconditionally.

What is completely surprising to me is that Lonnie said he never had bad dreams. With all the hazards around him, with the precarious nature of his life, with alcohol and illness and, as he noted, the danger of profound loneliness—he never had bad dreams. They were always beautiful and, he said, "informative." What did he mean by that? Maybe he got insights from them that eluded him when he was awake. Maybe his mind worked more efficiently when he was asleep.

I have bad dreams all the time. I have them in thematic strings—I'll have dreams about being lost, for example, every night for two or three weeks. That has been a recurring theme through most of my adult life. I am in a building I know but I can't find my apartment. Or I'm in a house where I live, and suddenly I discover that it has a second floor I didn't know about. Or I find an empty room in my house and try to figure out what I'm going to do with it. Those are fairly benign dreams, although they are unsettling and tend to linger through the next day. I've had dreams of being in car accidents, of people I love dying or going missing, of losing limbs, hair, or teeth.

Like Lonnie, I dream in color, and my dreams are sometimes informative. Once I had a dream that I believe was Dad communicating with me from the afterlife. It was intensely vivid, and I remember every detail. He and Mom and I were at the NASA Space Center visiting and looking at exhibits. There was a ride, something like a space simulator, that Mom wanted to go on. Dad and I agreed that our motion sickness prevented us from going, but we put her inside the model space capsule and stood watching as it bounced and lurched and swooped. Suddenly Dad turned me toward him, took my face in his hands, and said, "Tell your mother I didn't cheat on her." It was completely out of context in the dream, almost an intrusion, which made it feel all the more as though Dad had pushed into the dream to give me that message.

There was a period during their marriage when they were not getting along—"not relating," as Mom put it. Dad was working as manager at a company recreation facility and golf course. He was the *ex officio* social director and, being handsome, personable, and the tennis instructor, he was often around admiring women. Naturally he made friends with some of them, especially the ones who could give him a run for his money on the tennis court. Mom had a hard time, often wondering if some of those relationships were beyond friendly. She continued to wonder long after Dad passed away. When I told her about the dream, I prefaced what I said with a disclaimer that I knew it was going to sound weird, but that I was convinced it was genuine. I'm not sure how much impact it had on her suspicions. For me, it was perfectly informative.

Lonnie ended this card humorously, saying that, speaking of animals, he planned to be a clean animal the next day. He must have had an invitation to someone's home for a shower, or perhaps a local shelter or church had a scheduled shower day for the homeless. He sounds pretty enthusiastic about it. He noticed that he had misspelled "tomorrow" and made a joke about the error. Just thinking about his happy, colorful dreams put him in a good mood.

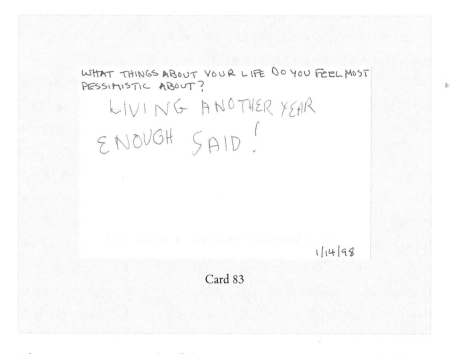

WHAT THINGS ABOUT YOUR LIFE DO YOU FEEL MOST PESSIMISTIC ABOUT?

LIVING ANOTHER YEAR

ENOUGH SAID!

1/14/98

Card 83

The way Lonnie tossed off this answer was eerie yet typical of him. He said it, but he didn't want to dwell on it, probably for his own sake as much as for mine. It lent a tinge of reality to his sunnier cards: clearly, he was not oblivious to the hazards of the life he chose for himself. But it made my persistent question—why doesn't he change it?—all the more perplexing.

January 1998 marked nearly 10 years since Dad died. Lonnie had been knifed, run over by a truck, mugged countless times, not to mention suffering the seizures that took over his body whenever alcohol withdrawal kicked in. Lonnie was still walking but relying heavily on a cane. Our Christmas visiting routine was unchanged, but it was about the only time I could get to Houston and see my brother. I was a full-time seminary student in Atlanta and working part-time as a freelance writer. I was too poor and too busy.

I wondered what might be on Lonnie's mind to make him answer this question so emphatically. He hadn't mentioned any particular issues to Mom, and when she had last talked to him (whenever that was), he had sounded sober and sunny.

This was one of the hardest things about being so separated from him. He could drop this kind of statement on me and I would have no way at all to put it into context. There was no calling to ask what he meant, no checking with a sister-in-law, not even finding out from Mom, who might not have heard from him in a month or more. Our lives, so intimately intertwined at the deepest levels, were almost entirely severed at the day-to-day level. There was no getting or giving advice. There was no going to his family's house for a Fourth of July cookout. There was no handholding as we waited for test results. The relationship was schizophrenic. In one respect, we were two halves of a single, shared life; in another, we were strangers. Each of us was in a relationship with a loosely reconstructed version of the other, based on ancient memories, fantasy, and the little secondhand updates that came, at best, monthly.

His reminder of the fragile nature of his life also reminded me that he could die in any number of anonymous ways and it might take weeks for us to find out about it. The best-case scenario would be if he died at the VA hospital. Lonnie borrowed Mom's address and phone number whenever a form asked for his permanent residence and contact information, so I knew they would be able to find her. I asked the nurses to add my name to his records many times, but I never knew whether the information lasted from one hospital stay to the next. He might die somewhere behind a dumpster or on some abandoned porch, clubbed over the head one time too many. He might have a seizure and simply not be found until it was too late.

I talked to the police at the storefront station about this and gave them my contact information. That way, I believed, if they found him, they would know to contact me. I hoped it would also mean that, if Mom and I went an uncomfortably long time without hearing from him, they could share whatever they knew about his latest status. In reality, they could tell me for certain where he was only if they had just hauled him to county jail or called an ambulance to take him to the VA hospital. But it was better than nothing.

In my relationship with Lonnie, there was a lot that was "better than nothing."

WHAT THINGS ABOUT YOUR LIFE DO YOU FEEL MOST OPTIMISTIC ABOUT?

THAT I CAN HELP OHRER PEOPLE OUT HERE WHEN THEY ARE HAVING PROB— LEMS BIGGER THAN MINE.

1/14/98

Card 84

Pregnant teenagers, drug addicts, runaways—these were the people Lonnie talked about whom he saw as having problems bigger than his. He wanted to help. He wanted to believe he had something of value to give—advice, care, testimonials, insider tips on living on the street—something only he could provide. He talked to the kids at the Covenant House about his life as an alcoholic on the street. He was willing to be the "this is how you could end up" example, and he had the charisma to get through to kids who tried to be tough and unreachable. That was Lonnie in his teens, but he wrapped all his rebellion and defiance in a personable, attractive package, making it look like nothing more than boyish mischief. He had that kiddish side all through his life, right up to the end. I don't doubt that the residents at Covenant House saw the kid in Lonnie and found him easier to listen to than most adults.

People without socks were another group of people with problems worse than Lonnie's. Every Christmas, Lonnie distributed the socks Mom and I always gave him to the people who gathered around the car when I dropped him off at his corner. They not only had no socks; they had no sister or mother taking them to another world for Christmas. They had no relief from the street. Lonnie had his imagination, which was muscular and unlimited, and it could take him to an infinite selection of worlds, times and lives. But he had reality, too—Mom, her house, her voice. He had me. And he had the postcards.

In January 1998, I was in the middle of my seminary education. I was swimming in debt already, but I was oblivious because I was so happy to be a full-time student and to have a clearly defined purpose for my days. I loved my classes, I read more than I had to, wrote more than I had to. I was learning theology, with a vertical learning curve that had to do with faith, joy, and what it meant in my life to be a disciple. In the context of what I was learning, and especially my experiences at the soup kitchen, Lonnie's answer on this card shines with a bright and piercing light. I had asked him what he was most optimistic about, wondering whether he felt optimistic about anything at all. His answer was that he hoped to help other people who had worse problems than his.

This says a couple of things that startle me. First, he believed he could help. He was uneducated, penniless, homeless—but he had no doubt that he had something to give. Second, he didn't regard his own issues as burdensome. I still shake my head over this. Here is how I think he saw it: He was strong enough to get around, able to see and, more or less, hear. He had a family who loved him. He had no money, but also no responsibilities, no schedule, no demands. Beyond all reason, his life made him happy. In fact, his life apparently made him feel lucky.

As a seminary graduate, I would say he felt "blessed."

8

March 1998

The jail characters Lonnie depicts on this card may or may not be real, but they are believable and instantly imaginable. (I am especially caught by the "cook that sells food"—an opportunist who holds meals for a ransom.)

WHAT'S IT LIKE TO BE IN JAIL, AT BEST? AT WORST?
IT DEPENDS ON HOW LONG YOU GOT.
THE BEST—A GOOD FRIEND, WHO IS
ALOT LIKE YOU! MAIL! A LIBERAL
PASTOR! GOOD COOKS DOING LIFE!
THE WORST—A SADOMASOCHISTIC TANK
BOSS! NO MAIL OR VISITORS! A
PUNK CELL MATE! A NAZI PAS-
TOR & A COOK THAT SELLS FOOD!
BELIEVE ME THEY ARE ALL THERE!
Write more on other side if you want

Card 85

These sketches sound like composites of people Lonnie had met in his dozens of trips to the Harris County jail, or in Huntsville State Prison. He lays them out as though he were making a pitch for a movie and this is the cast. For Lonnie, unsurprisingly, what makes jail good or bad is the people. Not the food, or the restrictions, or the cramped space and lack of sunshine.

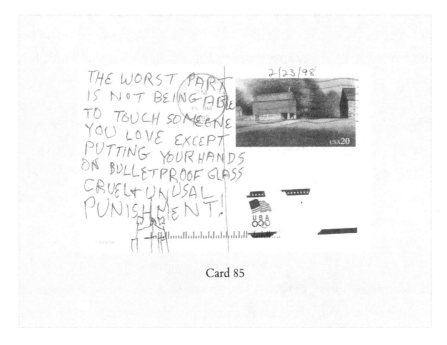

Card 85

After some thought, he pinpointed "the worst": not being able to touch someone you love. He made a tiny sketch of the scene that moviegoers recognize as the poignant moment between the inmate and the inmate's loved one, where they press their hands to opposite sides of the visiting-room Plexiglas and peer at each other.

I don't think this scene played out at county jail, where the visits took place in a room with plastic tables and chairs. The charges that landed people in Lonnie's wing of the county jail were relatively harmless—public intoxication, disturbing the peace, public urination, or trespassing. Visitors could, within reason, embrace.

After being convicted of "aggravated robbery"—Lonnie insisted that the gun he had carried in the convenience store robbery was carved out of soap—he was sent to the Texas State Prison in Huntsville. Visits were more restricted there, and closer to what Lonnie described. I visited Lonnie in prison only once. I lived in New York at the time, and when I was in Houston for a visit, I mentioned wanting to see him. Mom and Dad were hesitant about making the drive to Huntsville, and I probably didn't press the point too hard. I have always been pretty fearless about hospital visits, but jail and prison are another matter. A human confined behind bars is an unnerving sight, made more so by my mild claustrophobia and the thought of being so utterly under the control of someone else. I have that in common with Lonnie. Knowing Lonnie's passion for living outdoors, I saw this form of punishment as especially cruel for him. I wrote a song about it—sincere, intense, and naïve—about how his music would allow him to defy captivity.

We made the drive, and I remember that visit clearly. I had to talk to Lonnie through the bars of his cell. I wanted to hug him, but the guard watched us closely and jumped to move me back as soon as I approached the cell bars. It was uncomfortable and scary, and it made me angry.

I realize that Lonnie's postcards contain few complaints about jail or prison. His self-image as a free spirit—living on the streets, surviving by his wits, sleeping under the stars—is at odds with his appreciation for the safety and comfort of a few nights (weeks, months, or years) in jail. In fact, he thrived on the structure in Texas State Prison. He played in the famed Huntsville prison band, he learned data processing, and he was sober and reasonably healthy.

His "at best" scenario is a fairly accurate sketch of what Lonnie didn't have on the street, except, maybe, for the liberal pastor. Good friends and good food were pretty much out of the question, so if he got lucky and had a good friend and a few decent meals in jail, it was definitely a step up. Throw in a comfy cot, no mosquitoes, and taking a shower every day, and the time he spent in jail looked like pretty good time—at its best, anyway.

Card 86

Dad used to say, "If wishes were horses, we'd all take a ride." He was an Okie, and expressions like that came naturally to him—not that he authored them, but he collected them like verbal knickknacks. Lonnie and I inherited them. I still hear myself using them, even though Dad has been gone more than 30 years.

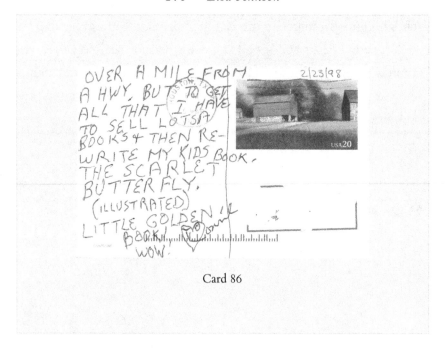

OVER A MILE FROM
A HWY, BUT TO GET
ALL THAT I HAVE
TO SELL LOTSA
BOOKS + THEN RE-
WRITE MY KIDS BOOK,
THE SCARLET
BUTTER FLY,
(ILLUSTRATED)
LITTLE GOLDEN
BOOK!
WOW!

2/23/98

USA20

Card 86

Dad had participated in some anti-authority behaviors of his own, especially in the Army. Among other things, he went AWOL to date Mom. He had an independent side that made him adventuresome and creative, and he was prepared to do whatever he wanted to do, whether or not other people thought it was appropriate (or sane). He joined the National Guard in his 40s, after losing his job at Armco. Even his superior officers noticed the 40-something guy who could do pushups and chin-ups along with the 20-somethings. As his contemporaries hit their stride in their careers, settled into family and community life and slowly developed middle-age spread, Dad was hard as nails (his phrase) and jumping out of airplanes.

Much later, in his 60s as he battled cancer (and slowly lost), he decided it was time to get the motorcycle he had always wanted. He bought it, but he was so weak he could hardly hold it up. I have photographs of him with his motorcycle, looking frail everywhere except his face, which sports a self-satisfied grin.

Mom was no stranger to inappropriately timed lifestyle changes. She got a sudden hankering for a career at age 55 and landed a job with a Houston real estate developer as community manager of one of their new residential properties. She ran the recreation facilities, supervised the maintenance staff, taught tennis, and demonstrated that the skills she had described in her interview, based on managing a household for 30 years or so, were honed and effective. As her contemporaries settled into grandparenting and bridge clubs, Mom conquered the corporate world.

And it was no coincidence that the job she accepted was in the same field as the one Dad held at the time. Dad was managing an employee recreation facility for a large, prosperous, oil-related company. He ran a golf course, tennis facility and clubhouse, teaching tennis, supervising the staff, and coordinating tournaments. He had been in an engineering position, but without the benefit of a college degree in engineering, his skills grew obsolete. He was a good worker, though, and well-liked by his manager and colleagues. When the position of club manager became available, they turned to him. He was successful in the job—it seemed tailor-made for him. Mom enjoyed great success in her job, including regular kudos from her supervisor and just-as-regular raises. The competition between them was spirited, especially on Mom's side.

What's missing from Lonnie's wish is the work aspect, the area where Mom's and Dad's wishes skewed them away from the "normal" course of adult life. Lonnie always wanted to make a living as a musician—he regularly told Mom and me that he had a recording contract with this or that studio and he was going to make his first million when the record went platinum. But that wish was no part of his vision of life by the creek. In its place was this book, and his children's book, which would sell a lot of copies and provide money for acreage, a truck, and a mobile home.

Lonnie's wish is almost identical to what I wish for, and what most people wish for. He'd be married to (not living with) someone who *really* loves him. (The emphasis is Lonnie's—*really* loves him, not pretends to love him, or only likes him, or doesn't love him as much as he loves her.)

Mouse *really* loved him. He said so on an earlier card, and he knew it was true. Their daughter, too, *really* loved him. Mouse finally had enough of Lonnie's irresponsible behavior—drinking, staying out all night, not showing up for jobs—and he gave up trying to shoulder the responsibilities of a family. They divorced, but Magda said she hadn't stopped loving him. Much later, he married a second time. His bride was girlishly beautiful and about 20 years younger than Lonnie. She loved him as much as her youth allowed. Her parents finally prevailed, and she filed for divorce after a year or two.

As far as I know, Gloria was the next (and, I think, last) great romance of his life. They were close for several years, but never married. When Lonnie asked her, she threw him out (according to Lonnie), later revealing that she had been married all along. (He reports about this in detail on the next card.) Cheating was something Lonnie never did. It was unthinkable. Like Dad, Lonnie was charming and handsome, and women were attracted to him. But, like Dad, he confined his extramarital philandering to flirting (even if it was occasionally the outrageous kind).

He said he would like to try to be a daddy again. He had the names picked out, and they linked his child to me and Dad. He didn't over-wish—he imagined only one child, almost as though he wouldn't risk the greediness of wishing for more.

His truck and mobile home on an acre by a creek a mile from a highway sound like a modern-day Walden Pond or Tinker Creek. Thoreau chose a site that was within walking distance of a town so he could get supplies (and what little social contact he needed). Annie Dillard regarded Tinker Creek as more of a neighbor than a geographical feature. I think I would be happy living in the next trailer down from Lonnie, with someone who *really* loved me, and our child, who would be named Jessie Baker, boy or girl. Jessie was the first name of my Grandpa on Mom's side; Baker was the maiden name of my Grandma on Dad's side.

Reality poked into Lonnie's vision, but only in disguise. To get money, he said, he would sell lots of books (this one)—and rewrite his kids' book, The Scarlet Butterfly. It would be an illustrated Little Golden Book.

We grew up on Little Golden Books, and I'm always happy to see them on the shelves in bookstores. There are some differences—Disney princesses, Barbie, and SpongeBob SquarePants occupy some of the pages, and the books sell for way more than their original 25-cent price. But *The Happy Man and His Dump Truck* is still there, along with *The Poky Little Puppy* and *The Saggy Baggy Elephant.*

I don't know what the story of the scarlet butterfly was, but in Lonnie's mind, it had the potential to finance his imagined life. "Wow," he said, and maybe that was when he noticed the connection between wishes and work. I agree with him: I think it could have happened. I wish (I *wish*) he could have lived long enough to collect royalties and buy his mobile home.

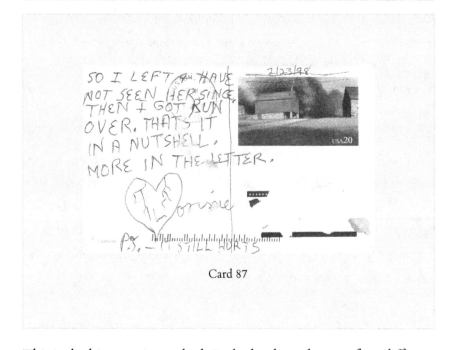

How did you come to be living on the street?
THERE ISN'T ENOUGH SPACE HERE.
GLORIA TOLD ME TO LEAVE AFTER
I ASKED HER TO MARRY ME. THEN
AFTER 2½ YRS SHE SAID "I THOUGHT
YOU KNEW I'M MARRIED" THEN AFTER
THE SHOCK I STILL LOVED HER, SHE
WOULDN'T DIVORCE HIM & HADN'T SEEN
OR TALKED TO HIM FOR 6 YRS.
BYE BYE BABY. NO LIVING IN SIN ECT.
Write more on other side if you want

Card 87

SO I LEFT & HAVE
NOT SEEN HER SINCE
THEN + GOT RUN
OVER. THATS IT
IN A NUTSHELL.
MORE IN THE LETTER.

2/23/98

USA20

P.S. — IT STILL HURTS

Card 87

This is the big question, which I asked at least three or four different ways and which Lonnie never really answered. Did he know? Had he forgotten? In his mind, he had come to live on the street after Gloria asked him to leave when he proposed. But he was already on the street when he started seeing Gloria, or shortly after.

What he did provide, though, were the painful details of what happened with Gloria. After two and a half years of being a couple, Lonnie proposed. Gloria's reply was to tell him to leave and, "I thought you knew I'm married." But he still loved her. He thought he might be able to talk her into divorcing her husband, especially since she hadn't seen him in six years. But she wouldn't do it, maybe because of the cost of a divorce, maybe because she didn't know where he was. So, unwilling to "live in sin," Lonnie left.

"Then I got run over," he added casually. Clearly the bigger event was the breakup with Gloria. The heart he drew and incorporated into his signature was broken in several places. The pain, as of the day he wrote this card, had not gone away.

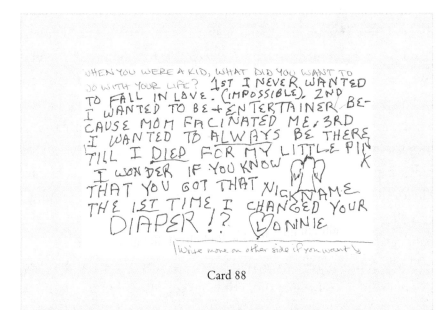

Card 88

Lonnie had been thinking about Gloria, reliving that hurt. In retrospect, he determined that, Number One, he had never wanted to fall in love. "Impossible," he added, meaning impossible not to fall in love, and his romantic history bore out this belief.

His Number Two brought back into the picture the music career that was absent from the dream life he painted so clearly on the last card. "I wanted to be an entertainer," he said, "because Mom fascinated me." Mom played piano and enjoyed giving concerts for friends and family. It was fun to listen and just as much fun to watch, as she was both beautiful and dramatic when she played, gazing off at times, playing without looking at the music in front of her.

Lonnie never had any music lessons—piano, guitar, or anything else—though he could have had them if he had expressed any interest. He preferred to simply sit down at the piano and start playing. His phenomenal ear enabled him to learn piano, guitar, and harmonica in just that way, and although he never became virtuosic on any of those instruments, he played well and wrote music of his own. (Janis Joplin's comment would have been true for Lonnie. She denied "writing" songs, saying she thought of it as simply making them up.)

The third thing he said he wanted to do with his life when he was a kid was to be there for his "Little Pink Angel" till he died. He said he gave me that nickname the first time he changed my diaper. That didn't happen. But according to Mom, he was crazy about baby me. He loved to hold me, and he played with me from the beginning, crawling around on the floor with me, walking me around by the hand, and helping Mom hang my diapers on the clothesline.

"Little Pink Angel" came much later, maybe when Lonnie was in junior high in Topeka and, while his grades started to sag, mine stayed aloft like so many gnats buzzing around his head. He started calling me Mom and Dad's little pink angel—I never did anything wrong and never got any grade below an A. Apparently, I was good at PR—when I look back at my report cards from that time, there were B's sprinkled among the A's. But compared to his C's and D's, especially after he had spent grade school in "A" territory, my A's chafed him.

"Little Pink" officially became my nickname when I started signing it on his birthday cards, and I didn't do that until we were adults. I thought it was funny, and Lonnie was tickled that I remembered and adopted the name he had used to make fun of me. As Lonnie's life became more tattered over the years, he used that name for me more and more. For him, it was a throwback to the life we lived together as kids. For me, I loved having a nickname that originated with him.

I know, and always knew, how much Lonnie loved me. Throughout his life, I never felt entirely disconnected from him. But that sense of connection was mostly a product of my need; there was little opportunity for us to "be there" for each other. I couldn't call him. I couldn't drop by his house for a cup of coffee or a beer. When other people talked about spending the Fourth of July at their brothers' houses, I wondered what that was like. When Mom was terribly sick, Lonnie wasn't there to help me handle it. When I got my cancer diagnosis, Lonnie wasn't there. When I graduated from seminary, Lonnie wasn't there. He was there only when he called Mom to report in. When he did that, Mom said, he always wanted to know how I was doing and asked her to tell me he loved me. Even that touching gesture wore thin over time. I resented having an absentee brother. Dad had been an absentee father when he was traveling heavily and had died when I was still in my thirties and nowhere near ready to live without him.

Siblings hold their shared childhood. What one sibling doesn't remember, the other does. The secrets, the perceptions of Mom and

Dad, memories of crazy relatives—the family stories, precious and unique, are carried jointly by siblings. Lonnie left and took his pieces of my childhood with him, and it happened long before he died.

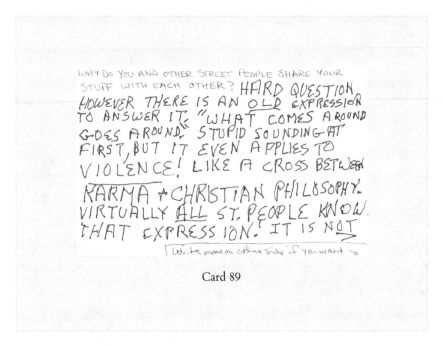

WHY DO YOU AND OTHER STREET PEOPLE SHARE YOUR
STUFF WITH EACH OTHER? HARD QUESTION,
HOWEVER THERE IS AN OLD EXPRESSION
TO ANSWER IT, "WHAT COMES AROUND
GOES AROUND." STUPID SOUNDING AT
FIRST, BUT IT EVEN APPLIES TO
VIOLENCE! LIKE A CROSS BETWEEN
KARMA + CHRISTIAN PHILOSOPHY.
VIRTUALLY ALL ST. PEOPLE KNOW.
THAT EXPRESSION! IT IS NOT

Write more on other side if you want

Card 89

He may have gotten the expression a little sideways, but Lonnie has the principle exactly right. In a sense, he's a strange one to be embracing a gospel of karmic payback. For example, the driver who hit him on the median as he sold newspapers never stopped and never was caught. On the other hand, Lonnie had alliances on the street, and someone who hurt him might "get hurt twice as bad" by friends of Lonnie's out for revenge.

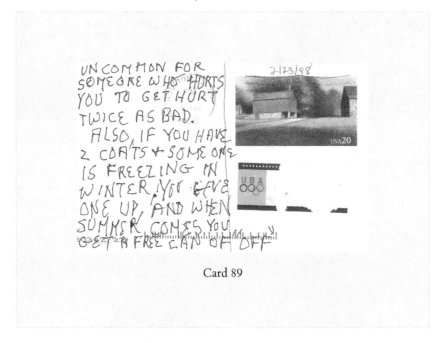

UN COMMON FOR
SOMEONE WHO HURTS
YOU TO GET HURT
TWICE AS BAD.
  ALSO, IF YOU HAVE
2 COATS + SOME ONE
IS FREEZING IN
WINTER, YOU GIVE
ONE UP, AND WHEN
SUMMER COMES YOU
GET A FREE CAN OF OFF

2-23/98

USA 20

USA OOO

Card 89

The principle of the two coats and the bug spray is one I saw in action many times, on many Christmases, when Lonnie dug the package of white socks out of his plastic lawn-and-leaf bag full of presents and handed them out to any of his street friends who happened to stroll by. Come the following summer, maybe one of them would remember those socks and lend Lonnie a can of bug spray.

Lonnie's life on the street seemed a lot more straightforward than my own. He needed food, water, a place to sleep, clothing, and bug spray. He had to survive. The people who used Lonnie's cane to hit him over the head, then stole it along with his backpack, were surviving. Lonnie was surviving when he positioned his wheelchair behind a car at the gas station and then slapped his hand on the trunk and tipped himself over. The driver would jump out of the car to see what the sound was (and maybe to see what damage the car had suffered). Seeing a guy lying on the ground, wheelchair next to him with its wheels still spinning, the driver would feel guilty—and ripe for Lonnie's request for a little cash. Survival didn't necessarily involve his conscience or heart.

It was a different way of surviving when Lonnie dug out his Christmas socks and gave them away, or when someone shared a beer with him, or gave him a can of bug spray. These were acts that would "come around" sooner or later, the karmic barter system that "all street people know."

HOW DO YOU FIND PLACES TO STASH YOUR STUFF?
PAWP TOLD ME WHEN I WAS
AS LITTLE AS A MAGGOT THAT
IF SOMETHING IS IMPORTANT
TO YOU THAT THE MOST OBVIOUS
TO YOU IS THE MOST INOBVIOUS
TO A THIEF. PLASTIC BAGS
& ROOFTOPS THAT I CAN REACH
W/ MY CANE ARE GENERALLY SAFE.
ALSO HEDGES (THICK) ARE GOOD.
OTHER THAN THOSE (OVER)
(Write more on other side if you want)

Card 90

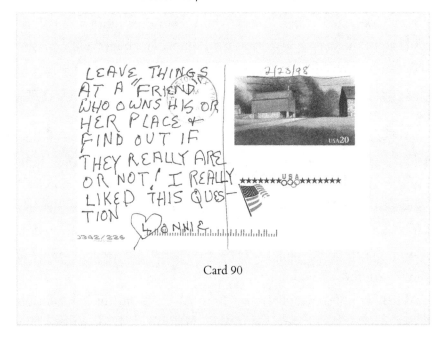

LEAVE THINGS
AT A "FRIEND"
WHO OWNS HIS OR
HER PLACE &
FIND OUT IF
THEY REALLY ARE
OR NOT! I REALLY
LIKED THIS QUES-
TION ♡ONNIE

2/23/98

USA 20

Card 90

Lonnie called Dad "Pawp," which was how Dad wrote "Pop." I don't know why he spelled it that way, and I've never known anyone else who spelled it that way. It was just him.

Dad never told Lonnie about hiding his stuff. Lonnie wanted to imagine Dad having that kind of role in his life, but it wasn't like that—at least, not much beyond Lonnie's sixteenth birthday. Before that, Dad had been a big part of Lonnie's success at football, scouts, even school. But as Dad's travel schedule grew heavier, his influence in Lonnie's life shriveled until Lonnie saw no reason to listen to him. They were adversaries throughout our family's stay in Topeka, getting into shouting matches, shoving and swatting at each other, and veering close to outright violence on a few occasions. (No wonder I grew so intensely close to my mother during this time: We were spectators to this unending clash between two people we loved.)

On several cards, Lonnie remembers Dad with incredible affection and admiration. But those feelings were rarely in evidence until

Lonnie was much older. I don't think Dad ever figured out what to do with the deep love he felt for Lonnie. His hopes and fantasies about his son faded when Lonnie became rebellious in his teens, and evaporated for good when Lonnie left the Army not "straightened out."

Dad was fired from Armco in 1968, and he had a hard time finding a job at an income level that would adequately provide for him, Mom, and me. Uncharacteristically, Dad decided to ask for help, and turned to Lonnie. Maybe Lonnie would consider moving in, getting a job, and contributing to the household income. Lonnie declined. It was not his thing, he said. Dad was humiliated and deeply wounded, and the rupture was complete.

When Lonnie's daughter was born, the frost in the relationship between Dad and Lonnie began to thaw. Dad adored his granddaughter. It's hard to imagine Dad's horror when she drowned—the loss must have shredded him. With Tookie gone, there was nothing to fortify Dad's tentative bond with Lonnie. Lonnie's downward spiral accelerated, and the distance between them was restored.

Dad let go of his anger and frustration, the disappointments and judgments, when he was dying of cancer. For Lonnie, that moment of forgiveness had been completely restorative. After Dad died, Lonnie's relationship with him was never better. Lonnie made the healing retroactive.

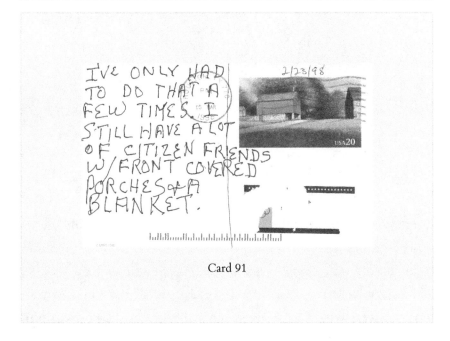

WHERE DO YOU GO TO SLEEP WHEN IT'S REALLY
COLD OR RAINY? VERY SIMPLE!
I CALL THE POLICE + COMP
COMPLAIN ON MYSELF, THEN
I GET DRUNK + WAIT. IF
THEY DON'T GET THERE SOON
I CALL AGAIN. IF THEY STILL
DON'T + ITS REALLY NASTY I
BREAK THE JUG IN FRONT OF
A CONVENIECE STORE. → LONNIE (OVER)
Write more on other side if you want →

Card 91

I'VE ONLY HAD
TO DO THAT A
FEW TIMES. I
STILL HAVE A LOT
OF CITIZEN FRIENDS
W/ FRONT COVERED
PORCHES & A
BLANKET.

2/23/98

USA 20

Card 91

It was kind of a relief to ask Lonnie a basic, straightforward question that didn't involve too much emotion. He cooperated, too, by giving me an earthy answer. If calling the police and complaining on himself didn't work—and why would it, as they probably came to recognize his voice?—he would "break the jug" in front of a convenience store. I had not heard that euphemism, but I later learned that it means he urinated. That would land him in jail.

But he went on to assure me, he hadn't used that trick often. More frequently, and more happily, he found covered front porches with blankets supplied by, as he calls them, "citizen friends."

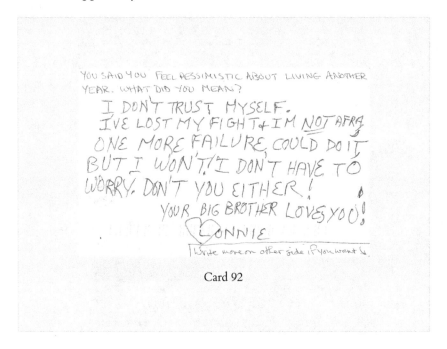

YOU SAID YOU FEEL PESSIMISTIC ABOUT LIVING ANOTHER YEAR. WHAT DID YOU MEAN?

I DON'T TRUST MYSELF.
I'VE LOST MY FIGHT + I'M NOT AFRA
ONE MORE FAILURE COULD DO IT
BUT I WON'T! I DON'T HAVE TO
WORRY. DON'T YOU EITHER!
    YOUR BIG BROTHER LOVES YOU!
        LONNIE

Write more on other side if you want

Card 92

I suppose when I asked this question, I was hoping he would say he was pessimistic about living another year because of his alcoholism, or because of his chronic bronchitis, or because he was always cold and hungry and in various forms of danger all the time. Any of those answers would have given me a springboard for urging him to get off the street, offering every kind of help I could. I never stopped thinking I could salvage him. I didn't see it as arrogant or misguided—I wanted us to be back in each other's lives, and I assumed he wanted that, too.

But "I don't trust myself" was nothing I could help with. "I've lost my fight" was ominous; "I'm not afraid" sounded like what people say when they are about to die. "One more failure could do it" was specific, like he had done the necessary calculations and was able to state conclusively how many more straws the camel's back could support.

But before either of us could think the unthinkable—that his life was about to kill him—he turned the corner. "But I won't" (fail, he meant), "I don't have to worry. Don't you either!" The disclaimer was as much for his own benefit as for mine, but the reassuring hug right before his signature—"Your big brother loves you"—was for me, the little sister. The big brother was supposed to worry about the little sister, not the other way around. I think it helped him feel stronger to remind me of his status as my protector. He returns to that image frequently throughout the cards—saying that Dad told him to look after Mom and me, or that he wanted to be there for me until he died. At times I felt like the big sister, looking after him. But "Your big brother loves you" was a set of words that I could lean into and feel like the safe, secure, little sister.

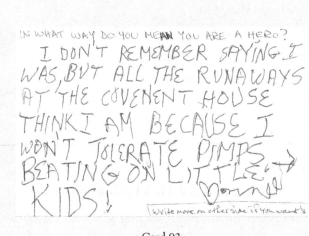

Card 93

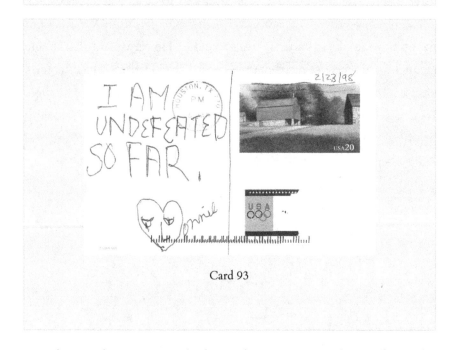

Card 93

On this card, Lonnie picked up the protective theme from the previous card and directly contradicted his comment, "I've lost my fight." On this card, he was "undefeated so far." But I notice that his writing is bigger and his thoughts more scattered. Judging by that, I would guess that Lonnie was working on a six pack while he wrote his answers.

All the same, he was right: He hadn't said he was a hero, he said he *wanted* to be a hero. But he did go on to say that the kids at Covenant House saw him as a hero because he wouldn't tolerate "pimps beating on little kids." This statement probably referred to something that had happened fairly recently. Unlike the story about the pregnant teenager whose baby Lonnie delivered, which he mentions several times over the years, the pimp reference made its only appearance on this card.

I have no trouble picturing Lonnie intervening if he saw a kid being bothered, much less beaten on, by a pimp or anyone else. Even in his wheelchair, he could be menacing, and wielding his cane he would have looked lethal and a little crazy. Lonnie had an affinity for the kids at Covenant House. They were the marginalized kids—thrown out by their parents, or desperate runaways, they were 18 or younger and seriously short of prospects. Many were addicted to alcohol or drugs; some were escaping enslavement to a pimp or a thug or a gang. He recognized feeling discarded, lonely, and hopeless.

On the back of the card, he added that he was "undefeated so far." But the heart he drew to sign the card looks sad and a little tearful.

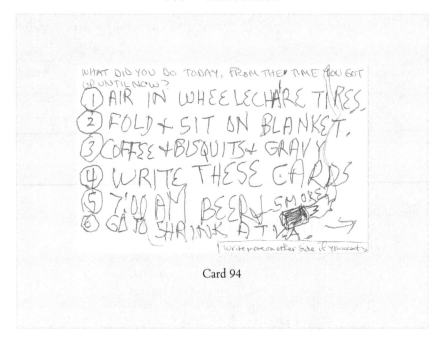

Card 94

This is the third card on which I asked Lonnie to recount his day in detail. He was up early on this day, and, before 7 a.m., he had put air in his wheelchair tires, rearranged his blanket to make it serve as a seat cushion, eaten his breakfast, and worked on answering the postcards. He mentioned "a beer and a smoke," which means, as I guessed, that he was drinking as he worked on the cards. He had (and it sounds like he kept) an appointment at the VA hospital to see a psychiatrist, probably for detox or anger management. But if he had the timeline correct, he went to the appointment fortified by beer. He mailed the cards that were finished. And "Anticipate nothing."

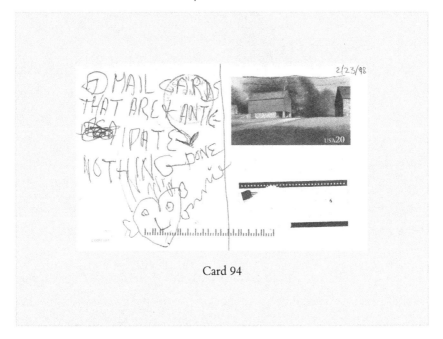

Card 94

Lonnie's life, in a nutshell. Tomorrow was irrelevant to him. He needed food right now. He needed to urinate right now. He needed a beer right now. He needed bug spray right now. Tomorrow would be identical, so why anticipate it, good or bad? An old Carly Simon song said that anticipation keeps you waiting, and for Lonnie, waiting was impossible. He had nothing in particular to wait for.

*   *   *

This was the last set of cards I sent to Lonnie. There was no definitive conclusion to the exchange. At the time of these last cards, I was finishing my second year of seminary, and I did as much freelance writing work as I could get that summer. By the time I started my last year of seminary, I was like a freight train slamming down the tracks toward graduation. I had the cards, I knew what I wanted to do with them, but I didn't do it until a few years later. I showed them to people along the way and told them about the idea. Over the years after I stopped sending the cards, Lonnie would ask me how the book was coming, and that would usually prompt a flurry of activity for a week or two.

After seminary, my life became incredibly disheveled. The ministry for which I had thought I was preparing did not materialize; that is, it materialized but didn't fit after all. I did freelance writing, but I was constantly looking over my shoulder longingly at the ministry career I had imagined I was going to have. I pastored a church in East Texas, failed, and moved to Houston in 2005. The year I made that move was the year Lonnie died of throat cancer, three weeks after his 58th birthday.

I visited him several times during his last stay in the VA hospital. He had a tracheotomy tube in his throat and couldn't talk much, but he managed to communicate fairly emphatically if he wanted to go out onto the patio for a smoke, or needed another pillow, or wanted his tray table rearranged. I had brought him a large photo of Dad, and one night when I walked into his room, he was sound asleep with both arms wrapped around that photo. I had also given him a little pink angel doll with kisses and hearts drawn all over her in magic marker; she was perched on his IV rack.

On one visit, he crawled out of his bed and arranged himself in his wheelchair, all the way at the head of the bed, bumping into the wall. I couldn't figure out what he was trying to do, but he gestured his answer. He patted the bed next to him, then smiled and placed his chin on his hand, waiting for me to take a seat where he had indicated and just sit with him.

The last night I visited him, he was asleep, or in a coma. He was breathing, but it was shallow and irregular. I sat with him for a while, crying and telling him how much I loved him. Then I got up, kissed him goodbye, and told him to go home. I wrote on the whiteboard at the foot of his bed, "Olaf, set sail." He died that night.

Mom was in the hospital at the time, with three or four things going seriously wrong. I took care of the paperwork for the VA records, claimed Lonnie's belongings, and handled the funeral arrangements. He had requested cremation, so I asked our pastor, a good friend of mine and Mom's, to go with me to the crematory. I didn't know what to expect.

The process was gentle and respectful. The funeral home representative wheeled in a small, corrugated-cardboard coffin containing Lonnie's remains. The box was secured with string, like an old-fashioned parcel headed for the post office. I had brought a small branch containing a few red berries, a reference to the poem I had written and given to Lonnie on a pocket-size laminated card. The poem told the story of a berry, first falling from its tree into the snow below, then, after a time, discovering that it was sprouting. I tucked the branch into the string, and then started walking around the box, talking to Lonnie, God, and myself by turns, telling Lonnie what he meant to me, thanking God for him, wishing Lonnie a safe journey, and reminding him to give Dad a hug for me when he got home.

When I had finished all I wanted to say, the director wheeled the cart and the box into the next room. Thick glass and a dark curtain separated it from the room where I had prayed. At my nod, the attendant pulled back the curtain. My first glimpse of the crematorium was jarring. It was a deep cement enclosure, rectangular but smaller at the far end, making it look deeper than it actually was. The first thought that came into my head was the empty tomb in Jerusalem, abandoned by Christ as he took his first steps into eternal life. It was a hopeful and even comforting image. Once my eyes had adjusted to what I saw before me, I nodded again, and the box was placed into the crematorium. I studied it, said goodbye, and felt an intense surge of gratitude. Lonnie was finally completely free from the body that had been ravaged by cancer, alcoholism, weather, knives, diseases, stinging insects, and a hit-and-run driver. I nodded again and the attendant closed the door on the crematorium.

I'm sure that Jesus pulled up in his black pickup truck, called Lonnie's name and invited him to join the party. This time, at last, I know Lonnie said yes.